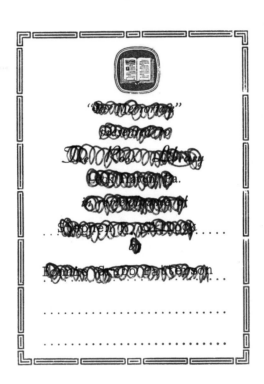

IN THE FOOTSTEPS OF MARCO POLO

IN THE FOOTSTEPS OF MARCO POLO

A TWENTIETH~ CENTURY ODYSSEY

HARRY RUTSTEIN AND JOANNE KROLL

A STUDIO BOOK THE VIKING PRESS NEW YORK

ISBN 0-670-39683-4

Acknowledgment
Selections from *Marco Polo: The Travels,*
translated by R. E. Latham. Copyright © Ronald Latham,
1958.
Reprinted by permission of Penguin Books Ltd.

Library of Congress Cataloging in Publication Data
Rutstein, Harry.
In the footsteps of Marco Polo.
(A Studio book)
1. Near East-Description and travel.
2. Rutstein, Harry. 3. Kroll, Joanne. I. Kroll,
Joanne, joint author. II. Title.
DS49.7.R87 915.6'0448 80-13964
ISBN 0-670-39683-4
Color printed in Japan by Dai Nippon Printing Company
Ltd., Tokyo
Printed in the United States of America
by The Murray Printing Company, Westford, Massachusetts
Set in Messenger with Gael italic

Contents

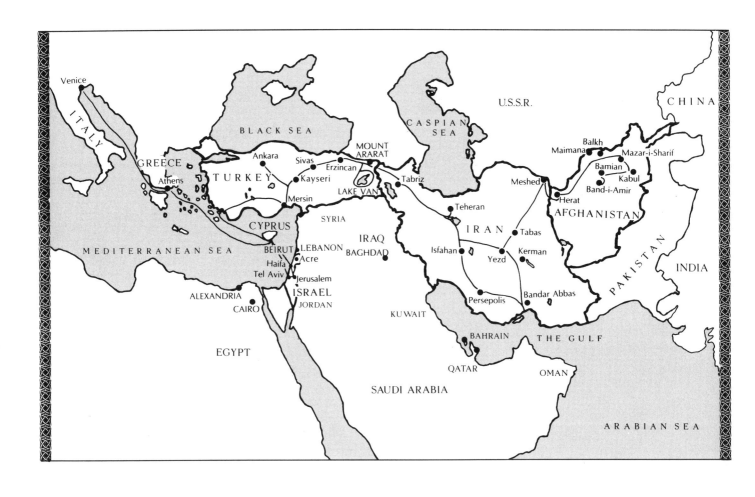

Foreword

As journeys often do, ours began in dreams and maps and books. It began in a love of travel, a desire to explore places where the descendants of ancient cultures live today much as their ancestors did hundreds and even thousands of years ago.

On July 20, 1975, we left Baltimore, Maryland, in search of the uncommon experience following a meandering trail across Europe and Asia to Peking, in the footsteps of the famous thirteenth-century traveler, Marco Polo.

In 1271 Marco, a youth of seventeen, made the journey with his merchant father, Niccolò, and uncle, Maffeo. No one has since been able to follow the route of the Polos in its entirety; not even the hardiest of ancient or modern travelers have succeeded. We were determined to try.

We wanted to document what we could of the culture and scenes in Marco Polo's world before the changes of the twentieth century alter irrevocably much of the timeless beauty and the tranquillity of these places; we wanted to experience ways of life that have endured through time, barely touched by the modern world.

Our Marco Polo expedition consisted of three travelers: Harry Rutstein, a Baltimore marketing executive, appropriately a merchant, who spent four years researching the tales of Marco Polo and planning the journey; Harry's nineteen-year-old son, Richard, who sought the excitement of travel in the Eastern world; and Joanne Kroll, an anthropologist from Cornell University, a professional artist, a registered nurse, and a lifelong traveler with a quarter of a million miles of experience in pursuing ancient cultures.

Starting in Venice, our group sailed to Acre, Israel, visited Jerusalem, and then went on to Cyprus and Rhodes, finally reaching Turkey by small sailboat in a storm-swollen Mediterranean. Local buses carried us across Turkey and the desolate Anatolian plateau past Mount Ararat, the hitching post of Noah's Ark, and south through Iran to the Persian Gulf. Just as Marco did, we in our twentieth-century odyssey retraced a few of our steps and again headed overland to the northeast, across the vast cloudless, silent deserts of Iran. We continued the journey into Afghanistan, following the Russian border for

Portrait of Marco Polo. From the first printed edition of his book. "This is the noble knight Marco Polo of Venice, the great wanderer, who describes for us the great wonders of the world that he himself has seen from sunrise to sunset, the likes of which have never been told." Courtesy Culver Pictures.

7

hundreds of miles, and then ended our travels high in the soft brown folds of the Hindu Kush mountains. In three and a half months we explored a route that took the medieval merchants nearly two years to travel. And this route was only the first half of the journey to Peking.

*M*arco Polo, his father, and his uncle went across Asia in the thirteenth century accompanied by servants, mercenaries, and mules. They carried letters from the Pope, and gifts, including fine vessels of crystal, water, and supplies, as well as a precious container of holy oil from the Church of the Holy Sepulcher in Jerusalem.

In the twentieth century what should we carry on a twenty-thousand-mile odyssey following the trail of Marco Polo across Asia? As little as possible! Especially since we would have to transport it all on our backs through a myriad of climates, from the scorching heat of the great deserts of Iran to the bitter cold heights of the Hindu Kush mountains in Afghanistan. Each item had to be weighed carefully in importance and ounces. In total, we took a modest one hundred and eighty pounds of baggage stuffed into three backpacks and three airline shoulder bags.

Internationally accepted currency was not available in the thirteenth century, so the senior Polos, Niccolò and Maffeo, had converted their merchandise into jewelry and gems. These precious baubles were easy to carry, and their fluctuating foreign exchange rate was a challenge to the Polos' ability to bargain. We used traveler's checks. These were exchanged for local currency at each border and at banks in the major cities.

The medieval travelers wrapped their belongings in a carpet or in heavy cloth, threw them across the backs of mules, camels, or horses, and proceeded across Asia. Although our method of travel was somewhat different from that of the Polos, our philosophy was the same. We traveled from town to town just as the Polos did, by whatever means available: sailboats, pack animals, buses, trucks, and always by foot in between; therefore some special considerations for packing were important.

During the early planning for the expedition

The Great Khan delivering a golden tablet to the Polo brothers. From a miniature of the fourteenth century. Courtesy Culver Pictures.

Joanne had suggested we find backpacks large enough to accommodate all our needs and protected by the toughest waterproof material available; everything was to be secured on the inside of the pack, including the tent and down-filled sleeping bag. She specified that the pack was not to have any outside appendages that could be used as a handhold, including a metal frame, except for the mandatory back straps. Her reasoning was based on years of experience in this type of travel. She had found that most bus, ship, or camel loaders invariably grabbed the weakest part of the pack while doing their job. All pocket and flap closings were to be fastened with heavy-duty zippers or straps and buckles. Drawstrings, often used on backpacks, were unacceptable, as they tended to work loose in the constant jostling. We finally found a pack that met these criteria, and others, such as light weight, padded straps, accessibility, and balance. The pack came in only one color: bright yellow!

The clothing needed for the desert was simple: cotton pants and shirts, a head covering, and heavy leather mountain boots to support our feet and ankles. To keep warm in the mountains of the world's attic in northern Afghanistan, the solution was also simple: we wore everything we owned. The hooded parkas, shells, and down-filled vests also helped. Emergency medical supplies, toilet articles, a three-month supply of toilet paper, flashlights, canteens, a collapsible water jug, and hundreds of safety pins as gifts for camera-shy people, all were to fit into our three packs. (The safety pins were the suggestion of Dr. Henriette s' Jacob, an art historian from Amsterdam, who had been traveling in Asia for more than fifty years.) A dozen travel guides and wall-size maps were important references and made good reading. No food was packed. We found our meals along the route, and we carried snacks in our pockets. Pistachio nuts, raisins, and dates were plentiful in most of the East. Two tape recorders with twenty cassettes, two Nikon cameras with four lenses, and one hundred rolls of film went along. Only exposed film and used tapes were mailed home to lighten our load.

We were fully prepared for wet weather, even though it did not rain from the day we left Venice

until we reached Kabul, Afghanistan, the result
of good planning and luck. Our packs were always
stored with those of fellow passengers. These
bundles, wrapped as they were in Marco Polo's
time, would often leak fluids, some familiar and
some strange, with indefinable aromas. On
occasion a harried helper would toss the luggage
into the sewage troughs that ran along the streets
of most Asian towns. Rain was only one reason for
waterproof packs.

Our journey came to a halt late in October 1975,
high in the Hindu Kush mountains, where the
valleys were at an altitude of thirteen thousand
feet. To the northeast the mountains are even
higher and the snows had already fallen, making
further travel along the old silk route
impossible. Marco Polo also stopped here in
northern Afghanistan because of an illness,
possibly malaria. He stayed a year. Marco
reminisces about his recuperation in the Hindu
Kush mountains in the following translation from
a sixteenth-century Latin manuscript by
Giambattista Ramusio:

*These mountains are so lofty that it is a hard day's walk,
from morning till evening, to get to the top of them. On
getting up, you find an extensive plain, with great
abundance of grass and trees, and copious springs of pure
water running down through rocks and ravines. In these
brooks are found trout and many other fish of dainty
kinds; and the air in those regions is so pure, and
residence is so healthful, that when the men who dwell
below in the towns, and in the valleys and plains, find
themselves attacked by any kind of fever or other ailment
that may hap, they lose no time in going to the hills; and
abiding there two or three days, they quite recover their
health through the excellence of that air. And Messer
Marco he had proved this by experience: for when in
those parts he had been ill for about a year, but as soon
as he was advised to visit the mountains, he did so and
got well at once.*

Sickness and war have impeded the movements of
travelers all through the centuries. The medieval
Polos and their modern-day counterparts were no
exception. They also found themselves thwarted
and delayed by these ancient adversaries. Today
traveling along the Marco Polo trail is in many

ways more difficult and even more dangerous than
it was a few years ago, and may prove to be an
impossible venture in the near future.

China was only a few hundred miles away, but
that government had sealed shut the back door to
its Sinkiang province in 1948. Someday we hope the
People's Republic of China will allow us to pass
through this fabled crossroad of Eurasian
civilization. We will then pick up the trail once
again and proceed, as Marco Polo did, across China
to Peking, the site of the Kublai Khan's winter
home.

Harry Rutstein
February 1980

Prologue

Emperors and kings, dukes and marquises, counts, knights and townsfolk, and all people who wish to know the various peculiarities of the various regions of the world, take this book and have it read to you. . . .*

The prologue of Marco Polo's book, known as either *Description of the World* or *The Travels,* continues with details of the voyage to Cathay undertaken by Marco's father and uncle eleven years before Marco embarked on his odyssey to the East:

In the year of Our Lord 1260, when Baldwin was Emperor of Constantinople and Messer Ponte governed the city in the name of the Doge of Venice, Messer Niccolò Polo, the father of Marco, and Messer Maffeo, who was Niccolò's brother, were in that city, having come there from Venice with their merchandise. They were men of good family, remarkable for their wisdom and foresight. After talking things over, they decided that they would go across the Black Sea in the hope of a profitable venture. So they bought many jewels of great beauty and price and set out from Constantinople by ship and went to Sudak.

After staying there for a while, they resolved to go further afield. Let me tell you about it. They left Sudak and went on their way and rode without encountering any adventure worthy of note till they came to the court of Barka Khan, lord of a great part of Tartary, who at that time was living at Bolgara and Sarai. Barka received Messer Niccolò and Messer Maffeo with great honour and was very glad they had come. The two brothers gave him all the jewels they had brought; and Barka took them willingly and was exceedingly pleased with them, and gave them goods of fully twice the value in return. These he allowed them to sell in many places, and they were sold very profitably.

View of the city of Venice in 1338. From a manuscript in the Bodleian Library. Courtesy The Bettmann Archive.

As they started back to Constantinople, Barka went to war, and the bitter fighting made the route by which the Polos had come too dangerous to travel. Niccolò and Maffeo decided to try to find a roundabout way home, eastward. They traveled to Bukhara in eastern Persia and remained for three

---

*Unless otherwise credited, the extracts in this book are taken from *The Travels,* published by Penguin Books; Copyright © Ronald Latham, 1958.

years doing a good business as traders. A Mongolian envoy from Levant came through Bukhara on his way to Peking and said that the Kublai Khan would be most interested in meeting the two Latins. The Polos saw a golden opportunity and took the long journey to China with him. They met the leader of history's largest empire.

The Kublai Khan, grandson of the ruthless Genghis Khan, sent the elder Polos back to Europe with an important mission: they were to return to him bringing holy oil from the Church of the Holy Sepulcher in Jerusalem and "a hundred learned men" to teach and introduce Christianity on a grand scale in the Mongol Empire. (No one knows the true reason for these requests, although they may have had something to do with the fact that the Kublai Khan's mother was a Nestorian Christian. More likely, though, the Mongol leader was seeking a political balance against the Buddhists. The idolaters, as the Buddhists were referred to by Marco Polo, were gaining a great influence in the court of the Kublai Khan.)

In Venice once again, the Polos found that Pope Clement IV had died, and there they waited for two years for a successor to be named. When in 1271 a Pope had not yet been chosen, Niccolò and Maffeo began their return journey to Asia, this time with young Marco. Word reached them, as they arrived in Lesser Armenia (southern Turkey), that Gregory X was the newly elected Pope. After an audience with him in Acre on the Palestinian coast, the Polos continued eastward. Pope Gregory allowed only two "learned men," both of them Dominican friars, to go with them, but the friars defected from the expedition in southern Turkey, in the city of Ayas, intimidated by the fighting then going on between the Egyptians and the Armenians. The Polos continued across Asia, carrying letters and gifts from the new Pope, as well as the holy chrism oil.

*F*or the purpose of this book the story of the Polos' journey through China and the years that they spent there will not be told. The twentieth-century expedition that set out to trace the Polos' steps ended by necessity at the back door of Cathay. It began in Venice and even before our arrival there.

Venice

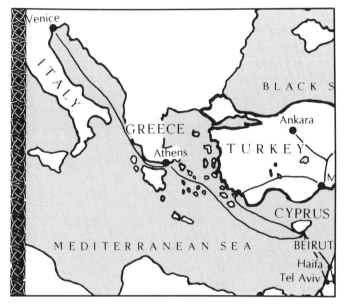

Venice at last, after years of planning, reading, and talking about the life and times of Marco Polo. Venice, home of this medieval traveler from birth to seventeen years of age and from the age of forty-one to his death in 1324 at sixty-nine. Venice in the thirteenth century was a great city-state that had acquired a mercantile empire controlling most of the major ports in the Mediterranean and Black seas. Venice, a city of islands that grew out of a lagoon. Venice, a city still living in the thirteenth century.

We found Marco Polo's first and second houses tucked behind an old church just a hundred yards from the Rialto Bridge, the only bridge that existed across the Grand Canal in the thirteenth century. One of the houses is a movie theater and the other, surprisingly, a hotel/pizza parlor. Our room at the Milabran Hotel overlooked the courtyard, which now serves as an outdoor café. The Marco Polo expedition could not have had a more authentic beginning than from a bedroom in Marco's original house.

The Rialto, where the Polos lived and the Venetians first settled in the ninth century, has always been the center of this city's commercial life. The merchants of Venice sat under the porticoes while their wines, spices, and precious Asian silks were displayed in nearby warehouses. Overlooking the Rialto Bridge were Europe's busiest money exchange and its famous bawdy houses, both ready to serve the hundreds of foreign merchants who came to do business in Venice. Farther along the Grand Canal is the Piazza San Marco (St. Mark's Square), the hub of Venetian social life. The tiled Piazza stretches from the eleventh-century St. Mark's Church, with its cupolas bubbling across the skyline down to the steps that fall into the blue lagoon. In this spectacular setting, guilds and religious brotherhoods would parade before the Doge, bearing banners and jeweled incense burners perfuming the salt air. The Doge, Venice's titular leader, celebrated his election there, scattering coins to the cheering crowds as he was

Opposite:

In the shadow of the back alleyway of what were once the Polo family stables the family crest is carved into the stone lintel above the doorway.

Marco Polo's home—today the Malibran Hotel and pizzeria.

Construction of St. Mark's Church began during the second half of the eleventh century, and by the time Marco Polo was a young man its structure had assumed the splendor that we know today. John Ruskin, the nineteenth-century artist/writer, described the roofline: "As if in ecstasy, the crests of the arches break into a marble foam, and toss themselves far into the blue sky in flashes and wreaths of sculptured spray, as if the breakers in the Lido shore had inlaid them with coral and amethyst."

carried by the craftsmen who built Venetian galleys in the nearby arsenal. This is the Venice that Marco Polo knew.

During the next few days at the Milabran Hotel we got to know Angelo Saivezzo, the manager, and his partner, Paolo Dorigo, who were very helpful with our exploration of the area Marco called home during his youth and after his return from Cathay. Mr. Saivezzo showed us a secluded courtyard and stable in which the horses of the Polo family were kept. Over the entrance to this courtyard was the seal of the Polos, which consists of three blackbirds on a shield. The shield is carved in the stone, with a knight's headgear and a scarf flowing in the wind chiseled into its background.

The courtyard beside the hotel is now called *corte dei Milione,* identifying the area by Marco Polo's nickname, "the millions." This was not a term of endearment, but one of ridicule, because this was the number he often used in his tales of the East. To the people of Venice, Marco seemingly could relate "millions" of stories, fantasies, and lies about that part of the world they did not know at all. Marco's book, known to us by either one of two titles—*The Travels* or *Description of the World*—related in detail what Marco saw and heard. It begins:

Emperors and kings, dukes and marquises, counts, knights, and townsfolk, and all people who wish to know the various races of men and the peculiarities of the various regions of the world, take this book and have it read to you. Here you will find all the great wonders and curiosities of Greater Armenia and Persia, of the Tartars and of India, and of many other territories. Our book will relate them to you plainly in due order, as they were related by Messer Marco Polo, a wise and noble citizen of Venice, who has seen them with his own eyes. There is also much here that he has not seen but has heard from men of truth and veracity. We will set down things seen as seen, things heard as heard, so that our book may be an accurate record, free from any sort of fabrication. And all who read the book or hear it may do so with full confidence, because it contains nothing but the truth. For I would have you know that from the time when our Lord God formed Adam our first parent with His hands down to this day there has been no man, Christian or Pagan, Tartar or Indian, or of any race whatsoever, who

*has known or explored so many of the various parts of the world and of its great wonders as this same Messer Marco Polo. For this reason he made up his mind that it would be a great pity if he did not have a written record made of all the things he had seen and had heard by true report, so that others who have not seen and do not know them may learn them from this book.*

It was many years after his death that Marco's book became the recognized geographical reference for the Orient and the key that opened direct trade between European merchants and the Far East. Up until this time all trade was conducted through the middlemen of the Middle East. Marco Polo reached the height of his fame in the fifteenth century and was in a way responsible for Columbus's discovery of America. Marco had become known as the greatest explorer and traveler in the history of the world. Columbus was envious and decided to outdo Marco Polo by finding a new, shorter trade route to China across the Atlantic. A well-worn and annotated copy of Marco Polo's *Description of the World* was among the books that Christopher Columbus owned when he set sail for the Orient and stumbled on America. It is now in a library in Toledo, Spain.

Along the brick and stucco walls of the hotel, the waters, strewn with garbage, lapped the edges of the canal. The singing of the gondoliers, clad in blue and white, interwove with the sounds of church bells and wailing babies and the animated conversations of late-night diners in the courtyard below. We could have easily imagined ourselves to be in Marco Polo's Venice—imagined it, that is, if we could have ignored the television antennas above us or the roar of motorboats speeding below our windows.

We walked across Venice toward the shipping docks, our luggage consisting of our packs and a small mesh bag containing bread, cheese, and fruit. There was no gold tablet from the Kublai Khan or document from the Pope, but the letters we did carry had been written by the ambassadors and cultural attachés of the countries we would visit as we pursued Marco Polo's trail halfway around the world.

Jerusalem

$\mathcal{L}$ike the Polos, we left Venice by ship and crossed the Mediterranean. The Polos sailed on a Venetian galley which landed in the now silted and shallow harbor of Acre on the north end of the Bay of Haifa in modern Israel.

From the deck of a Greek liner we watched: first, the Piazza San Marco and the rest of a brilliant pastel Venice drift past; then narrow islands and the beaches of the Lido; then we were in the Adriatic, with Greece and Israel ahead of us.

The sea was the deepest of blues and quiet, and the days went rhythmically by. We ate and we read. We watched an occasional school of dolphins off the starboard rail, and cribbage players in the lounge, and we talked for hours with our fellow passengers. There were elderly Greeks and a few young families, Costa, the cheerful bartender from Cyprus going back to work in his son's tavern, and an unhappy college professor from the United States, who talked of Mediterranean archaeology and remained just a little bit drunk throughout the journey. When his wife died he decided to give up twenty-seven years of teaching for a new life in Israel. There were Israelis and relatives of Israelis, and a vivacious young couple from Los Angeles, who had decided that there must be more to life than what's available in Beverly Hills. They had sold their home and were emigrating to Israel.

The people one meets on a ship like this comprise a diverse spectrum of humanity. There were a hundred shipboard faces to smile at, and a hundred stories to be told, and yet for the brief moment of a smile you were part of their lives. All this is part of the romance of traveling. This is what makes the inconveniences, indignities, and frustrations one faces all the more worthwhile. During those brief hours on ship many friendships are established that most likely will end as the boat reaches port, but the experience has been indelibly etched on each passenger's tablet of life.

Perhaps the Polos slept on the deck with the stars and with the sea mist in their faces as we

Opposite: *Brothers Niccolò and Maffeo setting out with their caravan, ca. 1270. From* Carla Catalana, *1375. Courtesy The Bettmann Archive.*

did, or ate bread and cheese and peaches with a little wine for the evening meal as we did. They surely did not lie late in the evening listening to the sounds of harmonicas and guitars and to the sounds of voices singing Greek and Israeli songs, songs that we soon heard only faintly as we drifted into sleep. The ship provided its own twenty-knot breeze, and sleeping was easy with the gentle rocking of the boat as its bow split the smooth Mediterranean, creating the soft sound of the spray as it drizzled back on us and the sea.

At about five-thirty in the morning of the second day we awoke to see sheer walls that we could almost touch on either side of the ship, and an enormous red sun rising from the pink haze directly in front of us. A tugboat was leading us through the clear waters of the Corinth Canal between the Peloponnesus and mainland Greece. We pulled ourselves out of our sleeping bags to watch.

It was about a sixty-minute tow through the canal and two more hours under our own power to the port of Piraeus outside Athens. We decided to take the excursion tour of Athens arranged by the ship. Our guide, Mickey, a dark-eyed, plump lady with a broad smile, gave a presentation that was not only knowledgeable but was full of national pride and was expressed in impeccable English. We visited the awe-inspiring Acropolis (literally translated, "high city"), where the ruins of many great structures still hold rein over this ancient city of Greece.

The Parthenon, or House of Virgins, is the chief temple and dominates the area with simple lines, pleasing to the eye and satisfying to the soul. It has served as a place of worship for all the many religions that have occupied this country over the past twenty-five hundred years.

The tour bus then took us through downtown Athens to the Archaeological Museum. There we saw the death masks that the father of archaeology, Heinrich Schliemann, found in the Mycenaean shaft graves: exotic black vases with red figures, "Linear-B" tablets with inscriptions that predated the Greek alphabet, hundreds of life-filled statues, and innumerable other artifacts from the Classic Greek Era. For all this we had only forty-five minutes—forty-five

Marco Polo's galley. Courtesy Culver Pictures.

minutes to absorb the work of a millennium. A lifetime would not be time enough.

On the third morning at sea we were told that the ship had stopped before sunrise off the island of Rhodes. We hadn't even heard the anchor chain roll out, although we slept only a few feet away from it.

On the fourth morning the ship slid into the humid, smog-filled, modern port of Haifa, not far from Acre but on the deeper side of the bay. We didn't have to pack. The ship's personnel had taken everyone's hastily repacked bags away from them late the evening before. Passport stamps, a formality unknown in the thirteenth century, were issued on the upper deck as we shuffled and sweated our way along with the throng of debarking passengers. And before long we found the local bus to take us to the area where the Polos had touched land, less than a mile away in Acre (Akko in Hebrew).

*I*nside the palm-fringed crenellated sea walls of Acre stone arches link ruined walls or straddle the dim and constricted streets. The fortress-like walls of the houses—Christian ones with a rare window high in the air, Arab structures sealed off from the outside world—testify to the millennia of invasions and occupations Acre has endured.

The Egyptians captured the city in the fifteenth century B.C., and Phoenician traders brought their vessels into the harbor three thousand years ago. Richard the Lionhearted and others sacked Acre in the name of Christianity during the Crusades. To quote from Marco's book, "For you must know that, when the Sultan of Egypt marched against the town of Acre and captured it, to the great loss of the Christians, this sultan of Aden contributed to his forces fully 30,000 horsemen and 40,000 camels, much to the advantage of the Saracens [Muslims] and the detriment of the Christians." Through the ages, warriors under many flags have waged many and bitter wars over this once critical center of commerce where the Western world meets the East.

In Eastern towns one rarely is allowed so much as a glimpse of the activities behind the blank walls of the dwellings—perhaps a child's face in

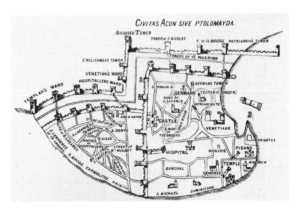

Acre as it was when lost (A.D. 1291). Some of the walls of Acre as shown in this drawing (made from a contemporary plan by Marino Sanudo the elder) still stand and many of the streets continue to follow the same meandering route. From Sir Henry Yules's Travels of Marco Polo *(1903).*

100830   ANNIE HALENBAKE ROSS LIBRARY
LOCK HAVEN, PA. 17745

JERUSALEM   21

a doorway or laundry fluttering high above the
street. We wandered along shaded cobblestone
paths and unpaved alleys or passed time in the
bazaars, for the pleasure of wandering and to see
something of the life of the communities.

In the Acre bazaar shouted conversations and
laughter and lovely, unfamiliar music greeted us.
Cries of "shalom" came out of doorways on all
sides as we meandered through the maze of lanes
and shops where splinters of light barely
penetrated roofs and canopies.

We could purchase, if we liked—and if we could
identify the object in the gloom—almost
anything: beige deck shoes or a finely handwoven,
hand-embroidered dress; a tooled leather camel
saddle or glow-in-the-dark paintings of the Last
Supper. We had a choice between silk prayer rugs
or more economically priced ones in
lively-colored plastics. Covered from head to
shoes with yards of dark, heavy fabric, elderly
Bedouin women with blue-tattooed mouths and
cheeks picked through the vegetables. The aroma
of freshly baked bread and of spices and goat
hides mixed with the smell of ammonia from puddles
of evaporated urine.

As we left the bazaar, in full sunlight again,
bands of clowning, unruly children danced in and
out of the shadows ahead of us and behind us. Some
had blue eyes and pale yellow hair; some were very
dark. All repeatedly arranged and rearranged
themselves in briefly serious and unsmiling poses
for our cameras. And then they continued
clowning.

A large herd of goats, tossing up thick puffs of
dust, accompanied us through the gate leading
from old Acre to the modern town. The goats
plunged into a nearby ravine. We boarded the bus
that returned us to Haifa.

For today's traveler Jerusalem is two and a
half hours by bus—a distance of 160 kilometers—
from Haifa. For the Polos the trip took as many
days.

*J*erusalem, once a Canaanite village, was
captured three thousand years ago by King David,
who made it his capital. In antiquity some called
Jerusalem the center of the world, although it was
and is located near neither waterway nor major

caravan route. Around the ramparts of Old
Jerusalem has grown a large and thoroughly
twentieth-century city. Within the walls of the
Old City are structures, the remains of
structures, and the widespread debris of
structures that were not new when the Polos made
their visit. The foundations of the immense,
substantial city wall are ancient, some parts
dating perhaps from the reign of King Solomon.
Sections of the original supporting walls of the
Second Temple remain; the rest was destroyed in A.D.
70 by Roman forces.

Although the mosque called Dome of the Rock was
converted for a time into a Christian church by
twelfth-century Crusaders, its form and much of
its decoration remain as they appeared when it was
built in the seventh century A.D. over the ruins of a
Roman Temple of Jupiter. Where once the walls were
crusted with mosaics, there are now sparkling
painted tiles, and the golden tiles of the dome
have been replaced with gold-plated aluminum that
can be seen for miles from Jerusalem hills. It is
from the site on which the mosque was erected that
the prophet Muhammad is said to have made his
visit to heaven on his horse, Lightning. The rock
in the mosque interior, for which the mosque is
named, was, ancient custom has it, the rock to
which Abraham came to sacrifice his son Isaac.

Also within the ramparts of the Old City, in the
Christian quarter, close to the bazaar entrance
and down an unmarked alley, is the Church of the
Holy Sepulcher, nearly hidden by the surrounding
buildings. Immediately as we stepped inside the
three-foot-thick-walled church, street noises
were no longer audible. Oil-filled lamps burned
at the head of a low, oblong sepulcher resting
over the traditional site of the tomb of Christ.
Investigating the deep and shadowed spaces around
and behind the lamplight, we saw that the church
interior is divided into chapels, some large,
some small, wooden scaffoldings alternating with
golden altars in dim recesses. In the chapels
prayers are said and masses are performed by
priests of the Greek Orthodox, Roman Catholic,
and Armenian churches, as well as the Syrian,
Coptic, and Abyssinian.

Near one chapel we met a soft-spoken gentleman
with kindly eyes and a dark beard. He was wearing a

deep blue cassock. With warmth and patience this gentleman, the Archimandrite Cyrill, of the Armenian church, answered our questions and talked of the history of this church and of the much-needed repairs and restorations that were taking place around us.

"The church is now much the same as it was in the twelfth and thirteenth centuries," he said, although, he added, minor alterations had been incorporated into the original structure over the years and "a wooden dome was destroyed by fire" and never replaced. He knew also of an oil which probably was the holy oil taken by the Polos to the Kublai Khan, "after it was blessed by the bishop"— "chrism oil," a mixture of balsam and olive oil used from antiquity to anoint kings, priests, and prophets.

There were workmen everywhere. But the peaceful stillness as we talked was hardly disturbed by the taps of the artisans' chisels as they carved ornamental stones to replace those lost or crumbling.

Outside the church everyone is concerned about Arab hostility. Radios blare at all times in public places and on the local buses, ready to announce a war and bring their military reserves into immediate mobilization. The buses have bars at the windows to prevent bombs from being thrown inside. Trash cans have unique covers that allow only small pieces of trash to be deposited. The mailboxes have metal strips across the openings, allowing only thin letters and postcards to be deposited. Anything thicker or larger must be handed directly across the post office counter. Guards at the entrances to every public building and every public area examine you and whatever you are carrying. The streets are continually patrolled by soldiers and police. One can easily distinguish between the two because the soldiers carry automatic rifles and the police carry handguns. Security is evident everywhere.

During a visit to a friend at the Israel Broadcasting Authority facilities, we asked the receptionist for directions to the engineering building. A scenario right out of a spy movie ensued. The guard-receptionist called for an aide to man his post at the desk while he walked the twenty feet to the door. He had taken a .45 caliber pistol from his desk. He cocked it, carefully looked around outside, pointed to the building with his left hand while he kept his gun hand in a ready position. This type of experience is now a part of everyday life in Israel.

From Jerusalem the Polos returned a final time to Acre for their visit with the Pope. They then set sail with their credentials, gifts, and the two fainthearted friars across the Mediterranean to the ancient port of Layas, in what is now Turkey. The Persian Gulf was their destination. The route through Ayas was a circuitous one, but it avoided wars being fought in the Levant by the Mongols.

The Gulf was our destination too, but we took an even more indirect route, as it turned out.

Cyprus

Today a sea route from Israel to Turkey no longer exists. For thousands of years vessels made regular sailings between the two coasts, but these sailings ended during the October War of 1973. From the eastern Mediterranean the modern-day Polo is told he can go to Turkey only by way of the island of Cyprus.

Cyprus is now, of course, divided, with almost half the island controlled by the Turks. Suspecting that we might have difficulties crossing from one zone to the other and finding passage across the sea, we called at a variety of consulates before we left Jerusalem. We wanted to know if it would be possible to continue the journey as we had planned.

Everyone was very helpful. At each stop we presented our itinerary and discussed it, and telephone calls were made to the appropriate embassies in Tel Aviv to ask the questions we had asked. At each stop we listened to declarations that it was indeed possible for us to continue with our plans, that there would be "no problem." We quickly learned that these two small words, heard frequently in the weeks ahead, were usually the precursors of our problems. But at this point we still retained our innocence. So we bought plane tickets to Larnaca in Greek-controlled Cyprus.

We boarded the plane, after a lengthy and extremely thorough two-hour security check in which random socks and assorted small items became mixed forever with the possessions of others and in which toothpaste and shampoo were tossed by the examiners into the backpacks with caps and bottle tops loosely replaced, if replaced at all. Capsules in our medical kit were opened and sniffed, cameras were clicked, tape recorders dismantled, and every part of our body and clothes thoroughly examined. Another passenger had the heel of his shoe removed in search of some sort of contraband. The guards found nothing, and the young man calmly hobbled down to the plane with his baggage, apparently accepting the inconvenience as a necessity for his own survival.

The flight from Ben-Gurion Airport outside Tel Aviv took one hour in an unair-conditioned Viscount. We perspired. The plane landed in Larnaca at 10:30 P.M.

We descended into the warm night, collected our bags, and went into the corrugated aluminum customs shed. We spread our passports on the counter and answered the questions put to us about how we intended to spend our time in Cyprus, and we were promptly informed that our plans would be not merely a problem—they would be impossible to carry out. After explaining to us what we could not do, the customs officer didn't know what to do with us or what to tell us that we could do. He placed a call to the Larnaca police station and asked to speak with the immigration officer, Sergeant Andreas.

Before long the sergeant himself was at the landing field, listening to our story. He was visibly upset with us for even thinking about going to the Turkish-held side of the island, much less discussing it with him. Again and again he reminded us that a quarter of a million refugees from the north of Cyprus had been forced to live in tents around Larnaca, some of whom were members of his own family, all of whom had lost their homes and most of their belongings.

But we continued to explain, and the sergeant continued to listen, and after a while he said that he understood and accepted our arguments and believed that our plans were peaceful and nonpolitical ones.

Still not happy about our need to get to Turkey, the sergeant tried to find some way to help us. He called the head of the immigration department in Nicosia and translated for us what he was being told on the telephone and what we had been hearing for ninety minutes: we could not go to Turkey from Cyprus. It was not legal and would not be permitted.

We knew that the new Greek-Turkish frontier was within hiking distance from Larnaca, and we had at one time talked of simply walking across this line and locating the ferry that would take us to Turkey. Anticipating this possibility, Sergeant Andreas quietly informed us that what we had been thinking about was also illegal and that if we wanted to attempt to leave Greek territory in this fashion we would most likely be arrested.

With this final caution—given with a firm invitation to visit him at the central police station in the morning—the sergeant at last asked the customs official to stamp our passports. He allowed us a twenty-four-hour transit visa, to give us "time to find an acceptable way off the island"—that is, through a Greek port. The Polos had managed to bypass politically turbulent areas. We had boarded a plane and flown directly into the center of one.

Perplexed and more than a little tired by now, we moved slowly into Larnaca and attempted to find a place to spend the one night we had been permitted to stay on Cyprus.

The town seemed to be asleep. We could hear nothing but the sounds of the invisible ocean to our right, and the only movement was that of bats flapping and diving through the light of the street lamps on our left.

Refugees occupied not only tents outside the town but also all the hotel space in Larnaca that was not filled by the few tourists. In other words, there were no rooms for us anywhere. The only accommodation we found was in the cocktail lounge of the Four Lanterns Hotel. The man at the reception desk turned on the lights in the lounge and said that what we saw was the best he could offer us. He brought two towels and a bar of soap and told us to make ourselves comfortable. We distributed our sleeping bags and our weary bodies on the dance floor and the stage—Joanne wanted to sleep on the stage—and quickly fell asleep. We were under not only the watchful eyes of the police but also of the amazed eyes of the early-rising hotel guests, who wandered through the lounge on their way to breakfast.

When we arrived at the police station early in the morning, everyone seemed to have been expecting us. The officers all knew who we were and where and how we had spent the night. Sergeant Andreas was waiting for us in his office at the top of the stairs.

The scene was a familiar one. We have all seen it in an old Humphrey Bogart movie at least once. We were on a hot Mediterranean island, seated, facing the glare of the sun, in a police official's office. Above us a large, slowly revolving fan barely stirred the dust in the still air. Palm branches hung motionless outside the open window. The sergeant was young and dark and handsome and had, fortunately for us, a friendly smile.

The sergeant offered us cigarettes. He ordered coffee and juice. He leaned back in his chair, lit a cigarette, and began to discuss our dismissal from his country. There was no indication or hint of the possibility of bribery as we had earlier expected. After a number of telephone calls and much conversation, the sergeant announced, "You are sailing tonight on a ship to Rhodes."

This was definitely in the wrong direction, six hundred kilometers to the west. But, he continued, we would have "no problem" finding a ship on Rhodes to take us to Turkey.

We expressed our thanks and farewells and joined three Cypriots in a hot, fast taxi ride along the coastal plain to the port of Limassol, about ninety kilometers away.

At the shipping office we discovered that there was already a problem. No one could sell us tickets because it was by no means certain that there would be room for us on the fully booked ship. But we could, the agent said, go to the pier at 10:00 P.M., at sailing time, and wait to see if there would be any extra space on the deck. There was, and at the very last minute we paid for our passage, rushed through customs, and ran up the gangplank to look for our piece of the deck on which we could camp for the night.

Unlike our eastbound trip on the same vessel

and on a calm, blue sea, the Mediterranean this
night was livid and stormy. Throughout the night
tall waves washed over the decks, and the wind
blew fiercely around the ship's stacks and
through the railings and cables. Sleeping under
the stars as we had done previously was not only
impossibly damp but impossibly dangerous as well.
This time there were many more people on board,
and below deck there was no place to sit, much less
to lie down.

*T*he following afternoon, after another ride
from the ship to the island by launch, we arrived
on Rhodes. As we gathered up passports and
backpacks in still another aluminum customs shed,
the official remarked that there would be no ships
to Turkey "for a while." Nor would there be for
another eight days a ship to Athens, from where we
could fly to Turkey. Only a short stretch of sea
separated us from the Turkish mainland, but
apparently we would not be progressing very
rapidly over it.

With these pieces of information we realized
just how tired we were after an uncomfortable
night. The backpacks felt heavy, and we became
suddenly and unpleasantly aware of the sultry air
and the blinding light from the sea.

Perplexed and discouraged, we trudged away
from the shed, along the concrete pier, toward the
town. And then—before we could think about
beginning to plan our next move—the three of us
sighted something that immediately lifted our
spirits: a forty-foot sailboat at anchor and
flying the red-and-white Turkish flag!

We made cheering noises. Harry dropped his
backpack, jumped over a low wall, and raced down
to the pier where the boat was docked. He asked the
tiny blond woman sunbathing on the deck, "Do you
know of any boats going to Turkey?" The answer
came in accented English: "Yes, we will soon be
leaving." The boat had been rented for a
Mediterranean cruise by six young Viennese, and
we saw them busily preparing to set sail within
minutes. After hearing the account of our
problems, they came to our rescue and asked if we
would care to sail with them. We were, to say the
least, ecstatic!

We were almost a thousand miles from our

planned route, but, just possibly, we were on our way to Turkey. Hitchhiking on a sailboat was not on our original itinerary, but why not? What could be more authentic than a sailing trip to Turkey, and were not the Polos diverted from their original course of travel by wars between and among the Seljuk Turks, the Mongols, and the Mamelukes of Egypt? After a dash back along the pier and through the customs shed for exit stamps and port tax payments, we once again set out to sea.

*T*he waters had been dark and rough the night before. They were no less menacing this evening. We sat on the afterdeck and sipped tea and watched waves half the height of the mast roll toward us. Then we watched them slip gently beneath the heaving hull. The auxiliary engine was straining to push the boat through the heavy seas.

Attila, the Turkish helmsman, fought the wheel to keep us from being swamped. With both hands the slender Attila gripped the wheel for hours without relaxing. Knowing, perhaps, that we watched and admired his skill, he infrequently gave the wheel a fast turn with two or three fingers. The tautness of his arm muscles betrayed the effort of this apparent offhandedness.

Increasingly distant, Rhodes faded away behind us. The misty purple mountains of the Turkish coast came into view. Isolated shore lights winked on as darkness fell.

And the boat engine coughed to a stop.

The three men who comprised the crew began shouting at each other. They ran from foredeck to afterdeck and in and out of the cabin and jumped into and out of the space below the deck—all in an attempt to restart the engine. Hidden somewhere until now because, the blonde told us, "he is afraid of the crew," the fragile-looking, aged, and toothless captain began calmly pulling the sails from their lockers.

On the edge of all this activity, we continued to sit where we had been sitting, fascinated by the lights on the shore which danced and whirled around us as the still fierce winds turned the boat in circles and nudged us slowly back into the open sea. We were also wondering just a little if anyone would know who or where we were if we were lost in all this black water. We wondered if waiting for the ship to Athens would have been, after all, such a bad idea. We wondered and worried and sipped another cup of tea for warmth.

An hour went by. Tempers and cylinders cooled. The crew stopped shouting and running. The shoreline ceased its dance. Attila was back at the wheel. The engine had started after the youngest member of the Turkish crew had poured boiling water in the battery. Near midnight we rounded a breakwater and slipped into a bay toward the cluster of twinkling lights that marked the little resort town of Marmaris.

At the dock the police, dozens of curious townspeople, and the tall, imposing owner of the boat, Mr. Karabenlis, welcomed us. We went into town after a quick stop at the police station, where we received amiable instructions to remain on the boat for the night and to take care of passport formalities in the morning.

Everyone—we three, the crew, the Viennese, Mr. Karabenlis; fourteen in all—celebrated our safe arrival with massive amounts of food at a waterfront restaurant. Platter followed platter to the table—fish and vegetables, shish kebabs and salads. Beer bottles were opened, and we toasted each other with *raki* (a strong, clear liquor that turns milky white when mixed with water) in English and German and Turkish.

We had, finally, arrived in Turkey!

Opposite: *The Church of the Holy Sepulcher, Jerusalem, was built in* A.D. *335 on the site of the crypt in which the True Cross was found. The church is now undergoing reconstruction in accordance with the original design.* Pages 34 and 35: *In the old city of Jerusalem, the gilt cupola of the sacred Muslim mosque of Qubbat al-Sakhra (The Dome of the Rock) adds a sparkle to the bleak desert/mountain skyline. The mosque was constructed in* A.D. *691 over the rock on which Muslims believe Muhammad rested his feet when he arrived at the end of his night journey from Arabia. Muslims remove their shoes before entering the mosque and are required by the Koran, before praying, to wash their faces and hands to the elbows and to wipe their feet to the ankles.* Pages 36-37: *An Arab child runs past the well in the courtyard of an Islamic* medresse *in Acre.* Page 38: *The great mosque at Acre was built in the eighteenth century by Jazzar Pasha. For thousands of years this biblical city was the gateway for trade between Asia and Europe and was the Crusaders' last stronghold on the Mediterranean coast.* Page 39: *Stone arches straddle the shaded streets of Acre, where fortress-like walls of the Christian houses and the windowless Arab structures have evolved to shut out the millennia of pillage and plunder that this city has endured.*

Turkey

After the several nights we had gone without sleep and after our several beers and the *raki*, the bunks and sleeping bags on the boat looked very inviting. We could still hear music and voices from the town, the water slapping the pier. The helmsman, now quite drunk, laughingly, vigorously, noisily swabbed the deck until a voice pleaded, "Enough, Attila, enough!"

In the company of the police, Mr. Karabenlis, and our hosts, we returned to town early in the morning. We climbed a narrow flight of wooden stairs and knocked on a door. After a pause a young woman, the customs agent whom we had obviously gotten out of bed, told us to enter. She drowsily welcomed us to her house and her country while she opened and closed several desk drawers, looking for her equipment. She ceremoniously stamped our passports and showed no interest at all in the backpacks which the police had told us to bring with us.

After thanking our hosts and saying good-bye to our new friends, we seated ourselves near the harbor to wait for the eastbound bus. Arrangements for our bus trip had been made from Marmaris, on the southwest coast of Turkey, to Muğla, where we were to buy tickets to Aydin; we would change buses again in Aydin and head east to Mersin.

The bus went through limestone mountains rockier than the Rockies but weathered and rounded, with formations that were strange and forbidding. The narrow road was lined with eucalyptus trees and a red blossoming bush that followed the roadside for the next three hundred miles. On the bus to Aydin we traveled with a young Turk named Mehmet Ali Sayarer, who owned a tobacco and pipe shop in Marmaris, which, of course, specialized in meerschaum. He was a graduate economist from Ankara University. His family was from the area of Eskisehir in West Central Turkey, where the white meerschaum used in making pipes is mined. The pieces of meerschaum are usually only a few inches in diameter and are the remains of fossilized sea creatures that were buried by nature millions of years ago.

Opposite: *The monastery of the Whirling Dervishes in Konya, in south central Turkey. It houses an Islamic museum and the tomb of Melvana Celal E. Rumi, who founded the dancing religious sect just prior to Marco Polo's journey through Greater Armenia in 1271.*

The bus continued through scrub forest and over dry mountains, past tobacco and cotton fields and olive groves, past tiny villages with red tile roofs on mud houses.

The Turkish men, without exception, had thick, neatly shaped black mustaches, an old tradition going back to the days of the harem. The eunuchs, who protected the women of the harem, could not grow facial hair; therefore, the growth above a man's lips proved his masculinity. Most of the men in the major cities wore Western-style clothing, but walking through the streets of a small village was a different experience. It was like walking on the backlots of a Hollywood set of a nineteenth-century Wild West movie. The clothing worn by men in the villages consisted of suit jackets with narrow lapels, baggy pants, white shirts, and narrow dark ties. We often saw men working in the fields dressed in this same manner.

Outside the cities most of the women wore a sort of pants called the salvar: a large quantity of fabric draped from the waist, down and between the legs, and tucked in at the waist on the opposite side. Others wore long but standard skirts sewed together at the hemline except for the two places from which the legs exited, giving the same effect as the draped fabric.

The heat was more than uncomfortable at times, especially in the buses, where the windows were never allowed to be opened so much as a millimeter. We could therefore be assured that the "dangerous" moving air wouldn't enter and that no sickness-bearing spirits could join the passengers inside.

Apparently we were the only ones who found the heat oppressive. A chorus of male-voice protests began if there was even a suspicion of air flowing into the bus. The women seemed content, clothed in their voluminous, heavy skirts worn with warm stockings and pants and two, three, or more sweaters and the ever-present head scarf which has replaced the veil in Muslim Turkey.

One scorching noonday on the coast we watched a group of nomad women bathing in the sea. Each was fully, modestly covered with the flowing skirt-pants, a scarf, and a mountain of wool sweaters. Only their slippers had been removed and left at the water's edge.

As in many other parts of the world, an essential part of travel in Turkey is eating. One goes nowhere, no matter how long or brief the journey, without the required bag or basket of food. To refuse an offer of food or to eat only a small portion of that which is offered is to risk hurt feelings; or worse, the refusal can be considered a grave insult, even if one finished a large meal only fifteen minutes before. And although we never stopped trying to order small portions, most meals turned out to be enormously large. So we ate rice and chicken and eggplant and lamb. And then, with as much enthusiasm as we could, we ate the food proffered by those traveling with us: grapes, cucumbers, raisins, nuts, and more. Much more! Starvation was certain to be no problem.

We held out our hands at least once between stops for a cooling splash of the lemon cologne distributed by the bus "conductor"—a refreshing custom unique to Turkish bus travel.

Another essential of bus travel in Turkey is music. The bus drivers seemed to like it, even to need it, while traveling. The passengers tolerated it. We usually arrived at our destinations with throbbing headaches. Called, we were told, "*dolmush* [taxi] music because no one other than bus or taxi drivers would listen to it," the taped music was always played at brain-piercing volume. And it was always played.

Our travel plans, altered by our passage through Cyprus, serendipitously gave us the opportunity to visit places not exactly on Marco Polo's route: the Roman ruins of Hierapolis now in possession of a few Italian archaeologists and hundreds of bats, Pamukkale with its hot calcium springs where the ancients worshiped and which form white waterfalls covering an entire mountainside, and Konya, the city of the Whirling Dervishes.

The ride eastward took us through bleak fields of boulders, fields salt-crusted and gray; and through greened fields of corn and wheat and more cotton and tobacco. The green fields are irrigated, as they have been for thousands of years, by troughs and waterwheels and buckets. Men cut hay while their wives and daughters scrubbed clothes in the distance.

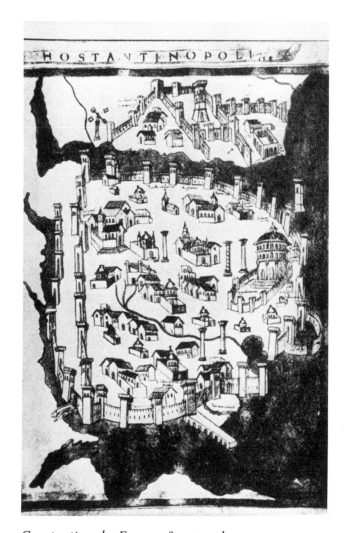

Constantinople. From a fourteenth-century manuscript; after Ptolemaeus, Geografia. *Courtesy The Bettmann Archive.*

The bus overtook and passed donkeys carrying straw piled three times their height, often with a child perched at the very top of the straw, waving and grinning as we went by. Undulating masses of gray and white sheep crossed the cracked, burned mountain slope, and their tiny shepherds—some of whom seemed to be little more than infants—scampered alongside the herds with their dogs. Dotted here and there were the brown felt tents from which the diminutive nomadic shepherds and the flocks had come.

And one humid evening we arrived at the west end of the Cilician Plain in the rather unlovely, modern seaport town of Mersin, near ruins of an old Roman port and near, at last, where the Polos had landed after their sea journey from Acre.

Arrangements had been made with the Turkish government to have a guide meet us in Mersin, and he was there waiting for us. Ertan Akbayar is an engineer by training, a photographer by preference, and a well-informed, enthusiastic guide. He is also a warm person and friend and an excellent cook, as we discovered when we stayed at his apartment in Ankara.

Ertan's welcoming and welcome gift to us was a much-needed Turkish-English dictionary.

Marco Polo tells of his arrival in Ayas from Acre. There is no Ayas in modern Turkey. Through research we found an ancient port and trading post which dates from the eighth century B.C., from the time of Hittite settlements in southern Turkey and from the later Greeks. This site, then called Aegae, became the chief port of Cilician Armenia. After several further name changes, and when it was no longer a port, the town was called in the nineteenth century Ayas, as were three other towns on the Turkish coast. Of the three we decided to visit the fishing village of Yumurtalik. The coastline here most resembles that shown on an ancient British Admiralty map we had copied of the old and once busy port. The map also showed a castle on an island a few hundred meters from shore. There was an island of this description at Yumurtalik.

Led by Ertan, we set off to see and to photograph Yumurtalik and to look for clues to its past. We were not disappointed. Almost immediately we found a section of a fluted Greek

Marco Polo's Ayas is the small fishing village of Yurmurtalik.

column buried in the wall of the ruined castle near the shore. And later in the afternoon more column drums and fragments could be seen protruding from the rubble of the town breakwater or lying loose and eroding beneath the waves. Further proof this was Marco Polo's Ayas.

On the sea coast lies the town of Ayas, a busy emporium. For you must know that all the spices and cloths from the interior are brought to this town, and all other goods of high value; and merchants of Venice and Genoa and everywhere else come here and buy them. And merchants and others who wish to penetrate the interior all make this town the starting-point of their journey.

While the others continued to search for an older Yumurtalik and for confirmation that it had once been the Ayas of which Marco Polo wrote, Joanne went off to explore the rest of the tiny, somnolent town. Few of the inhabitants were visible. Windows had been shuttered and doors remained closed. Most of the house and sea walls seemed to be turning to powder, bit by ochre-colored bit into the dusty lanes.

Paved road and the railway now follow Marco Polo's trail to Iran. With the guidance of Ertan we photographed and explored most of the towns along the old trade route.

We left Yumurtalik, traveling north to the area of Cappadocia, a wonderland where nature's fingers have clutched the fragile tuff stone and molded it into bizarre shapes, irregular pyramids, and surrealistic cones. Apartments were carved out of these cones by the Byzantine monks in the sixth century. Some are still in use today. Nearby is the city of Kayseri, where the trail turns to the east to Sivas. Marco Polo described this part of Eastern Turkey as follows:

In Turkey there are three races of men. The Turcomans themselves, who worship Mahomet and keep his law, are a primitive people, speaking a barbarous language. They roam over the mountains and the plains, wherever they know that there is good pasturage, because they live off their flocks. They have clothing made of skins, and dwellings of felt or of skins. The country breeds good Turcoman horses and good mules of excellent quality.

Woodcut of the Castle Ayas. From Colonel Sir Henry Yules's Travels of Marco Polo *(1903).*

The other races are the Armenians and the Greeks, who live intermingled among the Turcomans in villages and towns and make their living by commerce and crafts, besides agriculture. They weave the choicest and most beautiful carpets in the world. They also weave silk fabrics of crimson and other colors, of great beauty and richness, and many other kinds of cloth. Their most celebrated cities are Konya, Kaisarieh, and Sivas; there are also many other cities and towns which I will not enumerate, because the list would run to a wearisome length. They are subject to the Tartar Khan of the Levant, who appoints governors to rule them.

The landscape of Eastern Turkey was barren and treeless. Indeed, except in parks in the towns, trees were seen only rarely throughout the entire journey. The rock-strewn terrain was infrequently interrupted by green pasture or a patch of cultivated field.

There was, however, no lack of color wherever we looked. Snow-capped mountains in the distance constantly changed color from gold to brown to purple with the climb and descent of the sun in the luminous, clear blue sky. Donkey train following donkey train stepped alongside our bus; donkeys with grasses and brightly dyed bags, donkeys with clanking pots and pans and other multicolored household goods tied to their backs. Small and grimy children with their mothers led the donkeys. All were gaily dressed in velvets of reds and pinks and greens or in other shiny, colorful fabrics. White herons stood in the irrigation ditches, and rust-colored hawks soared overhead. Bright, tiny yellow birds flew up, then resettled on the shoulders of grazing cows.

Once in a long while we skirted small settlements of houses built of sun-dried bricks. These little dwellings huddled together with windowless backs turned to the road and seemed dwarfed by enormous stacks of hay and by large pyramids of drying animal dung that would be used as fuel for the fires in this treeless part of Turkey. Haystacks and dung hinted of the harsh winter soon to replace the heat that enveloped us as we traveled.

Again and again during the journey we had the sensation that time had long ago stopped its progress. Villagers stooped in the fields, swinging scythes, harvesting; huge hand-hewn pitchforks tossed and winnowed the dried wheat; yolked oxen plodded around and around, dragging a stone, grinding the grains, while other oxen carried off the yield; bent elderly men seated in blue-painted wagons with wobbling wooden wheels rumbled along the roads.

Marco Polo traveled as we traveled through Kayseri (ancient Caesarea) at the foot of Mount Erciyas to Sivas and across the River Euphrates to Erzincan and Erzurum. The arid land around Kayseri was crossed by dry riverbeds and speckled with the small white summer tents of nomadic shepherds. This rainless area gave way to flowing creeks and more agriculture as we neared Sivas, where fields and hills glowed golden with ripe wheat as far as we could see. Then the terrain, barren again, became red rock, then rugged, naked copper-bearing hills.

The cities were fairly modern, or trying to be, in a dusty, somewhat shabby fashion. Modern city or not, we found at every turn, often a few steps from an air-conditioned hotel, the very structures which the Polos also passed. Much of the handsome, bright Seljuk blue tiles and the chiseled stonework has endured on twelfth- and thirteenth-century buildings and on mosques and minarets. Domed, polygonal twelfth-century mausoleums sit between twentieth-century houses or stand stranded now alone on a grassy divider in a four-lane street.

Some of the mosques have been in use over the centuries; others are being renovated. The call to prayer by the muezzins still sounds thinly, quaveringly, from ancient minaret to minaret five times daily.

Active seven hundred years ago as theological schools (madrassahs), mosques, or hospitals, many buildings are now empty, elegant silhouettes against the sky, lovely shells, gray and silent. If the gates to the buildings have disappeared or have been left ajar, sheep and chickens let themselves in to graze or scratch at the ground in weed-filled courtyards where once students of medicine or of Islamic studies worked and slept. Intricate, delicate patterns in the tiles of the walls and ceiling vaults and intricate, delicate patterns in the honeycombed, high-relief carvings

that frame doors and windows suggest the past beauty of these symmetrical and still beautiful places.

We saw and continued to see carpets in a great variety of patterns and colors, carpets of wools and silks in all the hues one could dream of, carpets spread everywhere, from the rudest tent to the richest mosque, from bazaar floor to teahouse.

In Erzurum we had an opportunity to watch the process of carpetmaking at The School for Carpetmaking, Ataturk University, where girls begin at twelve years of age to learn the antique art.

A few of the students made kilims at the looms. A specialty of the individual villages, kilims are woven carpets in which the bold, color-filled geometric patterns appear on either side of the finished piece.

The majority of the students, however, practiced the more exacting, traditional method of making Turkish (or Persian or Afghan) carpets: knotting separately and by hand each wool or silk weft yarn on a wool or cotton warp. The weft yarn is twisted into a figure eight around two- or four-warp threads, tied, and cut, all in a blur of flashing fingers.

Only by looking carefully could we see much difference between the work of the novice students and those with more experience. The twelve-year-olds had before them smaller or simpler designs, and their fingers didn't move with the agility of those of the older girls, but their carpets were skillfully produced.

The school director, who showed us the workrooms and explained the girls' tasks to us, said that an experienced student could, in one minute, "make and trim perfectly with her knife about thirty-five knots," and that an advanced student working at this speed would complete a ten-meter carpet in about two years. Usually two or three girls sat before the work frames, rhythmically knotting and cutting, selecting a different yarn color when their drawings showed a change, creating the designs of these handsome, softly dark carpets. The school paid the girls three and a half Turkish lire per one thousand knots, or about twenty-five cents an hour.

From here we continued eastward.

In the town of Erzurum, the walls of the medresse *of the Twin Minarets are decorated with tiles in a design of stylized calligraphy.*

The art of carpet knotting has not been lost in Turkey. Schools such as the one in Erzurum where this photograph was taken are designed to keep alive the ancient craft.

Road to Ararat

*T*he bus left Erzurum on the caravan route that climbed and wound its way over the Tahir Pass at 8000 feet. Guardrails on these narrow roads are unheard of, and along the way lay memorials to those who had, once too often, driven the tight curves at high speed: carcasses of trucks and cars spilled down the mountainsides. "Allah will provide" is the fatalistic justification for not helping Allah just a little by driving with more care. Allah provided for us as our bus took the tight curves at high speed.

When we were safe again on the plain below, an army officer routed our vehicle off the highway and onto a path through harvested fields for a while. Nothing much taller or greener than a thistle grew along the way to Lake Van, but the cattle were abundant and plump so there must have been something edible somewhere. In the fields little boys carrying white cloth bags as large as they were gathered cow dung. We passed a bright red bus returning to Pakistan (so Ertan translated the banner on the side) from Mecca with a dozen Muslim pilgrims. The thistles and shrubs along a creek were festooned with the shirts and pants of the pilgrims, all male, who vigorously laundered themselves and their clothes under the afternoon sun. They waved to us as we passed. A baby howled at the world while his mother scrubbed his small body in a public fountain. Soon we saw a shining dot of water ahead.

Lake Van was a brilliant turquoise contrast to the tawny hills. We found a boat to take us the four kilometers to the island in the center of this high and saline body of water, lifeless except for a carplike fish.

The town of Van is an ancient oasis. It fell, over the ages, to the Medes and the Persians and, like every other place of importance, to the Mongols, but it survived. It survived, that is, until Tamerlane in the fourteenth century totally destroyed it.

In the tenth and eleventh centuries Van was a major town in the kingdom of Armenia, and here, early in the tenth century, on the bare rock of the island, a basilica, the Church of the Holy Cross, was founded. The building still stands,

The island of Aktamar on Lake Van. The Church of the Holy Cross stands on a rocky terrace in the midst of ruined monastic structures.

The well-preserved sculptures on the tenth-century Church of the Holy Cross depict scenes from the Old Testament: the story of Noah, the sacrifice of Abraham, the battle between David and Goliath; on the north side there are scenes of Adam and Eve, Samson, and Daniel in the Lion's den.

Faded frescoes inside the church.

golden-brown stone framed by the blue sky and the distant hills, alone in the lake except for gulls and mosquitoes and pigeons, and now us.

After a thousand years the interior fresco has faded, but one can still easily follow some of the painted scenes from the life of Christ around the dome. More clearly can be read the Bible stories cut in stone around the church exterior—among them Adam and Eve in the Garden, and an unhappy Jonah being pitched over the side of a boat into the waiting mouths of ugly beasts with doglike faces and the bodies of fish.

We climbed down the stony side of the island to the boat. As the late afternoon light started to fade, we watched the last bit of color being squeezed from the bald mountains: brown rust, gray, then nothing but shadows. The following morning we continued again toward Iran by bus.

The snow-covered peak of Mount Ararat came into view ahead of us, visible through the cloud of white dust in which we traveled and with which, floured and phantom-like, we had been smothered. Below us, in the northeast corner of Turkey, was the town of Doğubayazit, our last stop on the caravan route before we entered Iran.

Above the town on a mountainside sits a wonderful vacant palace constructed of red sandstone for a seventeenth-century pasha. The different levels of the building unevenly climb the hillside in a mélange of architectural styles, from Armenian to Seljuk Turk to pure fairy tale.

Balconies overlooked spacious gardens and courtyards. Carvings in stone and stucco twined thickly around and up every pillar and arch, and outlined the numberless windows, doorways, and spaces that appeared to be doorways but turned out to be windows. One discovers this when he throws open the "door" with foot poised to step forward into a space opening onto nothing but the mountain slope from two stories in the air.

Ceiling paintings had dimmed only a little, and the chains that suspended many dozens of lanterns still hung in place. We found interior balconies reached by hidden staircases, and cozy niches or tiny rooms set high in the walls from which one could watch unseen through filigreed screens the activities in the rooms below.

The untidy, dust-blown town of Doğubayazit had

The Palace of Abdi, a fairy-tale castle and caravanserai, presents an exquisite mixture of Armenian, Georgian, Persian, and Seljuk architectural styles.

nothing to compare with the romantic castle that looked down on it. Emaciated cows and horses stood here and there in the streets. Little was for sale in the market except a small and sad assortment of aging fruits and vegetables.

The thirty-year-old manager of our hotel, Fahrettin Kolan, had been a guide for expeditions that searched Mount Ararat for the legendary remains of Noah's Ark. At present non-Turkish climbers are not allowed on the mountain, and since most of the would-be explorers are not Turkish, Fahrettin hasn't led an expedition since 1972. He climbs now solely for his own pleasure.

He described for us the ascent on the east, "the easy" side of the mountain, as one would describe a pleasant three-day stroll. The climb on the north, on the "difficult side," he said, takes a good climber about a week over ice and snow. Son of nomads, a Kurd, Fahrettin spent the early summers of his life in the rich pastures halfway up the 17,000-foot mountain with his family and their herds.

His climbing methods might not appeal to the nervous or frail. He begins his climb, he said, in the dark of night "when the air is cool." "Tea at nighttime only" is all the fluid he allows himself, and he sleeps little—"a few hours, but not the first night." For supplies he needs only the tea and "a little chocolate, butter, and biscuits" and the single ski on which he makes his descent, "like the village children use in winter for sport."

The mountain, an extinct volcano, is called Koh-i-nuh, "Noah's mountain," by the Iranians. It has long been sacred to the Armenians, who have lived in this area for thousands of years and who believe that the ark does rest at the summit but that man has been forbidden by God to find it or see it.

As to whether any of the expeditions had learned something about the existence of the ark, or where it might be if it did exist on this mountain, Fahrettin admitted that no one had yet seen or found anything, but he related the traditional story that Marco Polo had heard and recorded seven hundred years before as he passed below Mount Ararat.

Mount Ararat's 17,000-foot peak probes the heavens and reigns majestically over hundreds of square miles in Turkey, Iran, and Russia. The ancient volcano is believed to nestle Noah's ark in its white glacial mantle.

Opposite and pages 58-61: *Cappadocia. The rock dwellings carved out of the cones in the sixth and seventh centuries housed Byzantine monks who came here in search of solitude. The paintings and graffiti on the interior walls have survived from the time of Marco Polo, and some of the "apartments" are still in use today.* Pages 62-63: *Sivas is a city of many beautiful monuments dating from the Seljuk and Mongol eras, the most outstanding of which is the Cifte Minare (The Twin Minarets), whose graceful minarets frame the elegantly carved portal of this old* medresse. *It was completed by the vizir Semsettin Mehmet in 1271, the year Marco Polo came to this central Anatolian trade center.* Page 64: *Not far from Mount Ararat, at the border of Turkey, Iran, and Russia, is the Palace of Abdi, a mountain caravanserai. These way stations along the Silk Route combined hotel, restaurant, mosque, and stable, usually within a single structure. The Palace of Abdi, built by a Kurdish chief, incorporates many forms of Islamic architecture.*

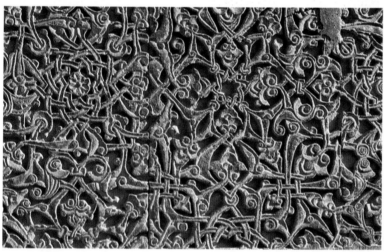

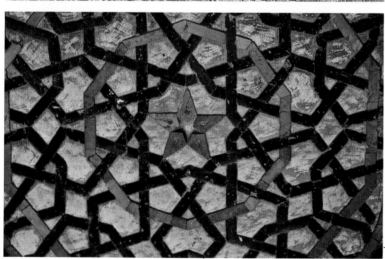

In the heart of Greater Armenia is a very high mountain, shaped like a cup, on which Noah's ark is said to have rested, whence it is called the Mountain of Noah's Ark. It is so broad and long that it takes more than two days to go around it. On the summit the snow lies so deep all the year round that no one can ever climb it; this snow never entirely melts, but new snow is forever falling on the old, so that the level rises. But on the lower slopes, thanks to the moisture that flows down from the melting snow, the herbage is so lush and luxuriant that in summer all the beasts from near and far resort here to batten on it and yet the supply never fails.

Fahrettin said that he too believes "that the ark is there, buried eighty meters down in the glacier on the Russian side of the mountain." He even drew for us a map of the area of the mountain and marked the supposed location of the ark. Is it only a long, long local tradition or a real possibility? Fahrettin wants very much to be able to climb again with those who want to continue the search.

About one hundred years before Marco Polo came to Mount Ararat, another traveler of the East passed this way, the Rabbi Benjamin Tudela of Spain, whose writings were translated from Hebrew into Latin in 1575. His story may hold the answer as to why the ark has not been discovered. The Rabbi writes about an Islamic leader, Omar Ben Al-Khataab, who removed the ark from the mountain and built a mosque of it on a river island four miles away.

Iran

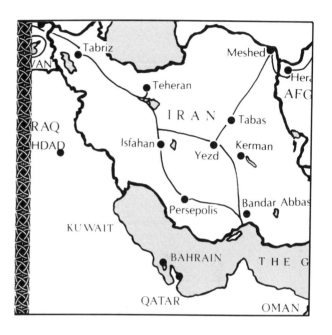

With Mount Ararat still in view behind us and trucks all around us, we said good-bye to our guide Ertan and crossed the frontier into Iran. Before us lay rapidly growing, rapidly modernizing cities. The landscape didn't change as we crossed the border. The hills were still treeless; where the land was irrigated, it was green; the rest was covered with patches of scrubby grass. The countryside was stark; when the hills became mountains, the vista was overpowering. Just across the frontier is the town of Maku; it sits at the bottom of a long gorge only two hundred yards wide. The mountainsides stand like giant jaws ready to take a bite from the blue skies. Mud-brick buildings seem to be glued to the sides of these canyon walls, and near the top is the ruin of a fortress. Beyond Maku the mountains spread apart as the road rolls along a level plain to Tabriz. Ahead of us was modern Iran and much of ancient Persia.

From northwest Iran the Polos traveled south through Yezd and Kerman and over the desert to the Persian Gulf. There they hoped to find a ship to take them to China.

In place of the Polos' "ship of the desert"—the camel—we rented a car in Teheran to carry us across the sands of Iran. The car would make up for the days we had lost getting from Cyprus to Turkey, and we would have more freedom to investigate less accessible areas of Iran. The car enabled us to spend time with many warm people we would not otherwise have met, but it also caused us to suffer a number of mild headaches and minor disasters.

Driving in the city of Teheran was an adventure story in itself. The trip across town from our hotel into the open countryside was as perilous as anything we had experienced. The car began to die before we left Teheran.

Malfunction succeeded malfunction as we followed Marco Polo's route. Retreating would have been as difficult as advancing, and more dispiriting. We could not remain where we were—on a narrow mountain road with oil-tanker trucks

Opposite: *The central courtyard of the Madraseh-ye-Madar-i-Shah in Isfahan. A marble water basin is enclosed by walls covered with richly colored mosaics of delicate flowers. The Shah Soltan Hossein, under whose reign these structures were built, took pleasure in the teachings of the mullahs of Islam and stayed at the college. Today the mullahs occupy the same cells that their predecessors did.*

67

scraping and speeding past in both directions. So we advanced, often very cautiously, from Teheran to Isfahan and south to the Persian Gulf.

*O*ccupied in the seventh century by the Arabs, Isfahan served as the capital city of Persia from 1051 to 1063, from 1072 to 1092, and from 1590 to 1722. Today Isfahan is sprinkled with architectural reminders of its long history. The city resembles a handful of jewels that some ancient giant set carefully in the desert.

It was long after midnight when we drove into town. Street lamps produced a muted amber glow that transformed the eroding mud and plaster of shop walls into works as golden and splendid as the domes of the mosques we passed.

The town was a treasury of soft-colored buildings faced with earthen color and pastel tiles. Even such mundane structures as twentieth-century gas stations had been covered with tiles of the same delicate colors. There were innumerable flower-filled gardens, innumerable fountains making rainbows with fine sprays of water that fell into basins and reflecting pools.

The Zaindeh River, invisible in the darkness below, was spanned by the simple, harmonious curves of yellow brick bridges gently illuminated in the night.

In the bazaar the following morning, smells and sounds enveloped us: the fragrance of herbs and fruits, saffron and vine leaves and pomegranate peel used to make dyes for the carpet yarns, the hushed sounds of bargaining, the greetings of people who ran a hundred yards to stop us and say, "Hello, how do you like Isfahan?"

Passing through dimly lit shops, past enormous vats of dyes and out the rear doors, we came upon courtyards crisscrossed with racks of newly, brilliantly dyed wools hanging to dry, or large yellow sheets of freshly block-printed cottons showing teahouse scenes and polo matches in greens, browns, and oranges.

Around the 1700-foot plaza, where polo matches and public executions once were held, women sat on benches in front of the shops, making carpets of silk with the pattern sketches tacked to the top of their work frames. In another shop we passed, very young apprentices squatted on ledges and rugs, with piles of thin wood strips and ivory and bundles of copper wire, gluing and piecing together inlaid boxes. Others hammered designs into sheets of brass and copper, embossing unattractive souvenirs for the tourists and more agreeably decorated kettles and samovars for Iranian homes.

A few steps from the covered bazaar stand the gifts of the Shah Abbas to Isfahan. All the numerous buildings commissioned by the Shah in the seventeenth century—mosques, theological schools, palaces—are works of rich beauty, each differing subtly from the other in colors and decorative themes, each with its own park or garden. Older buildings in Isfahan had been constructed of baked topaz-colored brick and of stucco with little ornamentation. The eleventh-century Friday Mosque and the later adjacent Winter Mosque are examples of this. Both were constructed over the foundations of Zoroastrian temples, and both contain large, dark spaces with low tentlike ceilings. A diffused light comes through sheets of alabaster, and the spaces are adorned with only the changing shapes and surfaces of brick and plaster. The feeling is one of warmth and utter tranquillity.

The Shah Abbas initiated in Isfahan the use of painted tiles. He apparently wanted to have built as many structures as possible and to have them built without delay so that he could enjoy them in his own lifetime. Because of the haste with which they were erected, many of the structures are in need of some or considerable renovation. There was no time to embellish the works with designs, which in a more leisurely period would have been composed of tiny mosaic tiles. Instead the designs were painted onto two-inch-square ceramic tiles, glazed and unglazed.

Entire walls, archways, and domes are covered with cut terra-cotta stalactites, painted rosettes and vegetal forms, or arabesques and scrolls of every curved and swirling decorative motif imaginable. The effect somehow remains controlled and tranquil. Colors and textures and designs catch and scatter the light, which changes with the movement of the shadows and brightens the unlit spaces with an iridescence like that from countless precious stones.

From the quiet interiors of mosques and madrassahs one hears only the most peaceful of sounds: birds calling outside the high, tiny windows, someone sweeping leaves from the walkways with a handful of twigs, at prayer time the whisper of carpets being pulled into place for the faithful to kneel on.

*T*he cannons boomed at dawn of our first day in Isfahan, announcing the beginning of Ramazan, the month-long period of pilgrimage, fasting, and prayer set by the Muslim lunar-religious calendar. We had been warned that it wouldn't be easy for us, non-Muslims, to find food and drink during this month, and it was true that most restaurants and market stalls remained closed until sundown, when the fast could be broken until sunrise. But, as usual, lack of food was not one of our problems. We continued to eat well and frequently.

The oasis of Isfahan opens into mile after mile of desolate, glistening white salt flats. We left trees and gardens behind us, except those we glimpsed through gates in the high walls of an occasional village. We passed the endless flats and cone-shaped mounds of salt and drove over the mountains in the direction of the Persian Gulf and into a blinding sunset sandstorm.

Increasing numbers of brown wool tents and camel herds appeared. In this area the nomads speak Turkish. The women are unveiled and exuberantly dressed in vivid, full skirts and gauzelike multicolored blouses trimmed with metallic threads. Ribbons and laces and velvet strips hang from every item of clothing. All the women have wavy hair swinging from beneath thin, bright head coverings.

The road to Shiraz took us near to Persepolis. Marco Polo may not have visited this spot, but we couldn't pass without stopping for an afternoon.

Now practically bare of vegetation of any kind, these hillsides were once heavily forested and were chosen twenty-five hundred years ago to be the site of the capital of the Persian Empire. Construction of the extensive group of works was begun during the rule of Darius I in the fifth century B.C.

Persepolis. Clockwise from top: *Along the side of the Grand Staircase the lion-bull decorative motif is artistically used in this triangular form, as it is in other ruins of Persepolis. Built twenty-five hundred years ago, Persepolis was almost totally destroyed by Alexander the Great in 330 B.C. / This bas-relief of the colossal winged bull with a human head is at the eastern side of the porch of Xerxes. / In the building called the Tripylon, the north and south doorways depict King Darius entering and leaving the palace escorted by two figures, one holding a sunshade and the other a flask of scent. The only other door to this structure leads to the Harem. / People from twenty-seven subject nations brought gifts to the great Persian kings, as this bas-relief of a bactrian camel suggests. This is one of hundreds of such bas-reliefs at Persepolis that describe the life style and culture of the ancient kings. Page 72: The fluted columns of the Apadana Palace.*

WD

All the structures rise from a vast elevated terrace. The east side is at the base of a mountain into which are hewn the tombs of later kings; the other three sides are contained by walls. To approach the halls and palaces, one climbs one hundred and ten stone steps on either side of a double staircase and passes through the columns that remain of Xerxes' gate.

Darius lived to see completed the ceremonial stairways and an audience hall that once had a sixty-five-foot-high ceiling supported by thirty-six stone columns; thirteen of the columns still stand. Successive rulers continued to add monumental architectural works: soaring pillars and gateways, a grand throne room, a profusion of megalithic slabs worn very little by time. The slabs are covered with reliefs of animals and of processions of gift-bearing representatives from distant corners of the empire, led by Medes and by Persians or watched over by the god Ahura-Mazda.

Never completed, the capital continued to be an important center for another six hundred years after it was plundered and burned by Alexander the Great in 330 B.C. Parts of the site were left under one or two feet of ashes. The empire was actually ruled from Susa or Babylon because of the mountainous and rather inaccessible location of Persepolis.

Persepolis existed mainly for show and for the celebration of the ceremonies of the New Year and the springtime reception of the gift-bearing visitors. The show was an awesome one if the immense and beautiful gray stones that remain are an indication; polished two thousand years ago, they still mirror the gold of sunsets and the honey-colored mountains.

We liked to think of ourselves as experienced and sensible travelers who would never, if we could avoid it, set off totally uninformed into the unknown. Especially if the unknown was a large section of Persian desert. In Shiraz we carefully inquired about travel conditions on our route south. The assurances came: the roads were "adequate" (we had in our hands a newly printed map that testified to that), and there would be "no problem."

Actually there was a problem. For miles and

miles and hours and hours we looked longingly at a thoroughly barricaded and as yet unpaved roadbed slicing across the empty landscape. Our path paralleled the would-be road—as far as the road went—as we plowed through the blowing, billowing blizzard of desert sand. Trucks had at some time passed this way. We occasionally spotted interrupted traces of their tracks in the shelter of a dune. Our delicate and dying Iranian Hillman in no way resembled a truck. As we struggled onward, the car slowly filled with desert sand and began to resemble a barely mobile sandbox.

Finally we came to within a few hours of the Persian Gulf. The strong, warm wind continued to blow from the south, and with our descent from the elevated plain the damp heat became swiftly and increasingly oppressive. A temperature of 130 degrees Fahrenheit is not unusual in this area. It probably was not quite that warm when we were there, but it felt like it. Our days and nights in Bandar Abbas on the Gulf left us feeling tremulous and vaguely weak in the uncomfortable outdoors, or fighting off frostbite in the icily air-conditioned hotels and restaurants.

The heat is so intense that the people of the area today take to the rivers for relief, just as they did in Marco Polo's time.

In summer [the people] do not stay in the cities, or they would all die of the heat; but they go out to their gardens, where there are rivers and sheets of water. Here they build arbors of hurdles, resting at one end on the bank and at the other on piles driven in below the water, and covered with foliage to fend off the sun. Even so, they would not escape were it not for one thing of which I will tell you. It is a fact that several times in the summer there comes a wind from the direction of the sandy wastes that lie around this plain, a wind so overpoweringly hot that it would be deadly if it did not happen that, as soon as men are aware of its approach, they plunge neck-deep into the water and so escape from the heat. To show just how hot this wind can be, Messer Marco gives the following account of something that happened when he was in these parts. The king of Kerman, not having received the tribute due to him from the lord of Hormuz, resolved to seize his opportunity when the men of Hormuz were living outside the city in the open. He accordingly mustered 1600 horses and 5000 foot-soldiers and sent them across the plain of Rudbar to make a surprise attack. One day, having failed through faulty guidance to reach the place appointed for the night's halt, they bivouacked in a wood not far from Hormuz. Next morning, when they were on the point of setting out, the hot wind came down on them and stifled them all, so that not one survived to carry back the news to their lord. The men of Hormuz, hearing of this, went out to bury the corpses, so that they should not infect the air. When they gripped them by the arms to drag them to the graves, they were so parched by the tremendous heat that the arms came loose from the trunk, so that there was nothing for it but to dig the graves beside the corpses and heave them in.

In this district they sow their wheat and barley and other grains in November, and they have got in all their harvest before the end of March. And so with all their fruits: by March they are ripened and done with. After that you will find no vegetation anywhere except date palms, which last till May. This is due to the great heat, which withers up everything.

The cantankerous camel is as much a part of the desert and desert travel today as it was when Marco Polo traveled. The Arabian camel is primarily a beast of burden, though it also provides hides, meat, milk, and wool.

The final part of the journey to the coast was uneventful. We enjoyed the scenery as much as we could. Through the glowing haze of the heat everything seemed to be slightly out of focus and pink-tinted: the hill and rock formations, the sand and sky. Antelope sprang across the road. A herd of camels crossed in front of us, leaving one female unmoving and staring disdainfully down at us from the center of our path. Had the car horn still worked we could have honked at her. She looked at us as long as she cared to, then moved leisurely off to the side, giving the car fender a deliberate thump with her right hind foot as she went.

The Polos had come to the Gulf at the old port of Hormuz (not the twentieth-century town of that name) to find a ship. They inspected the available vessels and decided that all were badly made and not seaworthy.

Their ships are very bad, and many of them founder, because they are not fastened with iron nails but stitched together with thread made of coconut husks. They soak the husk till it assumes the texture of horsehair; then they make it into threads and stitch their ships. It is not spoiled by the salt water, but lasts remarkably well. The ships have one mast, one sail, and one rudder and are not decked; when they have loaded them, they cover the cargo with skins, and on top of these they put the horses which they ship to India for sale. They have no iron for nails; so they employ wooden pegs and stitch with thread. This makes it a risky undertaking to sail in these ships. And you can take my word that many of them sink, because the Indian Ocean is often very stormy.

The Polos retraced their steps to the north and continued their journey to Peking overland.

Bandar Abbas is an increasingly active port, and the town is growing rapidly in size and population. But there is nothing there for the tourist, including hotel rooms. There are a number of hotels, all of which seemed to be overflowing with visiting salesmen, engineers, naval officers, businessmen, and transient laborers. Only a few years ago the population was about ten thousand. There are now about fifty thousand permanent city residents, plus another fifty thousand living in tents. In addition to the Kurds, Turks, and other Iranians, there were many people from India and Pakistan. It is once again an Asian crossroad, just as it was in the time of the Polos.

After a long and fruitless search for a place to sleep, we were offered lodgings in a telecommunications office next to a waterfront facility called the Welcome Inn. There were beds and there was a shower built for the hotel employees next to the kitchen. We could take a private, undisturbed shower by propping the door shut with soft drink cases.

We suspected that not many foreign tourists came to Bandar Abbas. The sign over the tourist office door was written only in Arabic script, and only one person in the office, Saadi Echrati, spoke any language besides Persian.

Mr. Echrati was invaluable in helping us find a place to have the car repaired. The car had been without a functioning horn or speedometer since we had left Teheran. It now had, among other problems, no brakes, no spare tire, and several unhealthy grating noises somewhere inside. Everything was taken care of with smiles and a speed and efficiency that left us speechless in any language, and minus a small sum of money: $4.38.

Maps in hand, we drove off to find the site of the old port of Hormuz.

Merchants come here by ship from India, bringing all sorts of spices and precious stones and pearls and cloths of silk and of gold and elephants' tusks and many other wares. In this city they sell them to others, who distribute them to various customers through the length and breadth of the world. It is a great center of commerce, with many cities and towns subordinate to it, and the capital of the kingdom.

Partially abandoned in the early part of the fourteenth century because of Mongol incursions, the port was relocated to an island two miles offshore. It remained active, especially in the export of salt, until 1622, when Bandar Abbas was founded by the Shah Abbas and Hormuz became economically less important.

The desert along the Gulf was flat, with little vegetation other than scattered strands of date palms, and little water except for an occasional green and dirty pool. Everything seemed to have been abandoned to dust and heat and depression.

Our previous research and the aeronautical maps we studied indicated that the small village of Tiab was near the ancient port of Hormuz. Mr. Echrati gave us directions to the town of Minab, one hundred kilometers from Bandar Abbas, and told us to ask there for directions to Tiab. We found our way to Minab even with the cantankerous carburetor in the Hillman limiting our power. In the Minab River flowing through the town, women bathed with all their clothes on and children with none. Just as in Marco Polo's time the bathers were joined by women washing their clothes. Not far away there were a few men scrubbing trucks and donkeys.

With more directions from the local people we finally found the road to Tiab. When we'd gone five or six kilometers along this sandy trail, we began to be more apprehensive. Not so much because of the perils of a large stretch of unknown desert but because of the threat that the car might give up running completely. With this concern in our minds, we were stopped by a riverbed that was no longer crossed by a bridge. Crossing now required a four-wheel-drive vehicle, and we were still

Landing of Marco Polo at Ormus. From Livre des Merveilles. *Courtesy Culver Pictures.*

driving the Hillman. Should we turn back? How important was Hormuz, and was it worth the risk?

We decided to go on. After all, this was not just a travel tour; it was an expedition to follow authentically and verify the route of Marco Polo across Asia, and Hormuz was an important way station in the thirteenth-century odyssey.

Where old Hormuz had been were just a few thatched-roof mud houses set on the muddy beach, with a few weathered gray disintegrating boats littering the shore. The town looked deserted and defeated.

The nearby town of Minab appeared to be as impoverished as the settlement at the old port site. Abdullah, a bartender in Bandar Abbas, told us that drinkable water and food were scarce in this area: "Not much more than dates and some goat milk or cheese to eat." While some of the adults seemed to be well nourished, most of the children we saw had large, rounded bellies and sticklike arms and legs. Skeletal beggars also lined the town's streets.

Because of the heat, not all Muslim women on the Gulf wear chadors, although they cover their bodies thoroughly with long-sleeved shirts and long, close-fitting, lace-trimmed pants under skirts. Instead of concealing their faces with veils, they wear fabric or leather masks—shiny reds, blacks, browns edged with lace, hiding all but glimpses of chins and dark eyes. The masks allow some air to circulate around the face and are in themselves pretty but give the women a strangely wolflike appearance.

Bandar Abbas is not a place where one would want to linger, and we soon, as did the Polos, turned to the north again.

Kerman

The return journey from Hormuz to Kerman passes through a fine plain amply stocked with foodstuffs. It is blessed with natural hot baths. Partridges are plentiful and very cheap. Fruit trees and date palms abound.

*T*he road to Kerman is paved. We climbed rapidly to the drier, cooler 6000-foot plateau through multihued, heavily eroded mountains.

Perched at the top of the turquoise-colored dome of this mosque in Kerman are Arabic quotations from the Koran. Marco Polo tells of turquoise stone produced in "great abundance" in this province. An ancient Persian legend describes turquoise as the color of the bones of people who have died of a broken heart. In ancient times buildings were often decorated with this soft blue color to ward off evil spirits, and the tradition has been carried on to this day by Islamic architects.

Tiab, a small fishing village, was once the major port of Hormuz on the Persian Gulf, funneling the wares of India and China to Persia and the West.

Opposite: *Men work at their trades in the Great Bazaar of Isfahan, where for hundreds of years one could find all the riches of the world, all the marvels of Persian craftsmanship.* Page 82: *Masjid-i-Jomeh (The Friday Mosque) in Isfahan is large enough to welcome five thousand people to prayer. Its buildings and decorations have been preserved intact from the Mongol and Turcoman periods. The honey-comb ceiling* (bottom left) *is from the Palace of the Forty Columns, on the great square of the Shah Abbas, Isfahan.* Page 83, left: *The Madraseh-ye-Madar-I-Shah (School of the Shah's Mother), in Isfahan, is crowned with a superb turquoise cupola guarded by two minarets. A canal within the courtyard of the school reflects its tranquility and multiplies its beauty. A jewel of Persia, Isfahan retains the opulent and colorful character that Marco Polo described.* Right: *The cupola of the Mosque of Sheikh Luftullah as seen from below its dome, and the mosque's decorative minaret.* Page 84, top: *Along the trail to Bandar Abbas a small shrine stands alone in the desert.* Bottom: *In the blistering hot town of Bandar Abbas water is stored in a covered mud-brick well.* Page 85: *The Hindu temple in Bandar Abbas, which was the major port of Iran on the Persian Gulf, was constructed to serve the many Hindus of India who had migrated here.* Page 86, top: *A teahouse in the city of Kerman, famous for its hand-knotted carpets.* Bottom: *The heat in Bandar Abbas is so stifling that married Muslim women wear a wolflike mask instead of wrapping their chadors across their faces.* Page 87, top: *Every community in the Muslim world has a mosque, each with its own character and beauty, from the sublime to the simple, like this one in Yezd.* Bottom right: *The minarets that stood in the center of the oasis town of Tabas were totally destroyed by the 1978 earthquake.* Page 88: *At the center of the sacred city of Meshed (The Place of the Martyr) is the mausoleum of Iman Reza, who died in A.D. 817. The religious complex includes many prayer halls, reception rooms, restaurants, offices, a hospital, a library, and—most spectacular of all—the treasury.*

Now let me tell you about an experiment that was made in the kingdom of Kerman. It so happens that the people of this kingdom are good, even-tempered, meek, and peaceable, and miss no chance of doing one another a service. For this reason the king once observed to the sages assembled in his presence: "Gentlemen, here is something that puzzles me, because I cannot account for it. How is it that in the kingdoms of Persia, which are such near neighbors of ours, there are folk so unruly and contentious that they are forever killing one another, whereas among us, who are all but one with them, there is hardly an instance of provocation or brawling?" The sages answered that this was due to a difference of soil. So the king thereupon sent to Persia, and in particular to Isfahan aforementioned, whose inhabitants outdid the rest in every sort of villainy. There, on the advice of his sages, he had seven ships loaded with earth brought to his kingdom. This earth he ordered to be spread out like pitch over the floors of certain rooms and then covered with carpets, so that those who entered should not be dirtied by the soft surface. Then a banquet was served in these rooms, at which the guests had no sooner partaken of food than one began to round on another with opprobrious words and actions that soon led to blows. So the king agreed that the cause did indeed lie in the soil.

It may be interesting to note that during the 1979 revolution Isfahan was the site of many killings, the sacking of public buildings, and continuous turmoil, whereas in Kerman not one major incident occurred.

Kerman is also famous for the brilliance of its starry nights as well as for its carpets and pistachios. Clouds and the city lights prevented us from appreciating the night sky. The deep-colored carpets are indeed handsome, and a fresh Kerman pistachio is infinitely more flavorful than the red-tinted nut available in the neighborhood supermarket in the United States.

Many of the mosques and madrassahs and portals of the Kerman bazaar were built after the fourteenth century. Even though some of the buildings are quite lovely, they generally lack the rich colors and forms of earlier constructions, and the glowing neon tubes spelling out "Allah" over the portal of a fifteenth-century mosque are quite garish.

Of more interest to the thirteenth-century traveler and to us was a tall structure, shaped like an inverted cone, at the edge of Kerman: an icehouse. Used in desert towns from antiquity, these large hollow cones are built with a wide shelf spiraling around the outside from the top to the ground and below, where the spiral opens onto a shallow trench. A thin layer of water is allowed to run into the trench, or moisture collects on the spiral and drips into the trench, where on cold desert nights it freezes. The trench is well protected from the sun's warmth by the thick walls of the cone. The ice is broken up and moved to caverns deep in the ground, where it is stored until needed. More water is run into the trench, and the process is repeated.

Often seen at the side of the icehouses, or seen around similar cones that cool and shelter drinking water, are towers called *badqirs* or wind traps. We saw them also on top of almost every house. Built of mud or mud brick, these *badqirs,* mentioned by Marco Polo, are further examples of adjustment to life in the harsh desert. Whether box-shaped or rounded, the principle of the various *badqirs* is the same: to catch the slightest breeze in the vents at the top (on one, two, or all four sides) and to funnel the cooling air down through internal, vertically placed wooden slats to the dwelling or water below.

*T*he towns always appeared unexpectedly as we crossed the Iranian plateau. The land is flat. The settlements are flat, and the dust and haze obscure what little might be visible otherwise in the vacant landscape. Much of the great interior plateau is unexplored. The plateau is called *kevir,* consisting of salt wastes or swamps—large areas with unstable salt crusts overlying mud. Here few people have wanted to venture, much less settle.

One suggestion that a town was somewhere ahead of us was the presence of *qanats.* Like giant molehills in a line, these openings in the sand are the entrances to shafts that lead below ground to water flowing from distant springs, through man-made channels, to the towns. Marco Polo spoke of seeing *qanats* in his travels, although he apparently thought they were natural formations.

An icehouse located about a mile from the center of Kerman. The inverted-cone-shaped building is about sixty feet high. Massive insulation and the continuous cooling waters that spiral down its side keep the winter ice stored there until summer.

The traveler arrives at a stream of fresh water that runs underground. In certain places there are caverns carved and scooped out by the action of the stream; through these it can be seen to flow, and then suddenly it plunges underground. Nevertheless, there is abundance of water, by whose banks wayfarers, wearied by the hardships of the desert behind them, may rest and refresh themselves with their beasts.

Inside the Zoroastrian Fire Temple in Yezd a priest led us to a smaller room in which this fire burns. Its flame has been dancing above the urn, it is said, for more than a thousand years.

We continued north until we saw the low, sand-colored, barrel-vaulted roofs that mark the town of Yezd, "a very fine and splendid city and a center of commerce," according to Marco. At the crossroads of many major caravan routes, Yezd has been from ancient times both a commercial and a religious center. Fifteen centuries after its founding, it continues to be commercially important, mainly in the manufacture of silk fabrics. As Marco Polo observed, "A silken fabric called *yezdi* is manufactured here in quantity and exported profitably to many markets." Yezd continues to be important to the Zoroastrians, those who still practice the religion of pre-Islamic Persia.

We proceeded to the Zoroastrian Fire Temple. After we covered our heads and removed our shoes, the young priest took us inside the small white building. A sacred fire burns in a brass urn set in the middle of a marble cell in the center of the temple. The fire is isolated from all except the priests and is carefully shielded from the direct rays of all external light, artificial or sunlight. This fire, the priest told us, has been changed five times a day for the past thousand years—that is, prayers have been said while new wood and incense are added to the urn and the ashes are removed. Although Zoroastrians are known as fire worshipers, the priest wanted to be certain we understood that this is a misnomer. "The fire," he said, "is an intermediary between man and God. For the followers of the prophet Zoroaster, the god is known as Ahura-Mazda. The fire is a symbol of truth and good, not the thing worshiped."

Outside of Yezd, in the desert, on a quiet, windy mountainside stand two stone towers, one of which is about six hundred years old. Unused since 1970 (at "government request," said the temple

priest), these towers, Towers of Silence, open at the top to the sky. The inner walls are arranged in three concentric circles on which the Zoroastrians for centuries placed their dead. Rather than, as their religion forbids, "contaminate earth, air, or water," the dead were dealt with by birds of prey—birds called "living tombs"—and the natural decaying of the dry, hot sun.

The religious beliefs haven't changed, but the authorities have insisted that the Zoroastrians bury their dead in the new cemetery below the towers. Few graves could be seen in this small, grassy space at the foot of the mountain.

Because of Ramazan, the shops in the Yezd bazaar remained closed throughout the day, and we encountered few people in the covered passages. But men continued to sit, hunched over, in gloomy, half-hidden rooms, weaving with silk yarns. The patterns of plaids and other simple geometric designs weren't very pretty, but the colors were, and the tedious work with the fine threads was impressive to watch.

As always, there were old mosques and madrassahs to explore and photograph, with the aid of old and toothless doorkeepers, who first helped Joanne to cover herself with a chador and then helped us all to find our way through the buildings. We found a prison, built during the time of Alexander the Great, which was being restored, the subterranean cells now covered and sealed, the structure above converted into a madrassah. Near the prison stood an empty but well-preserved ninth-century mausoleum protected by two young bulls munching hay, and a proud, grinning, very old man.

To reach what is now Afghanistan from Yezd, the Polos had to cross the Dasht-e-Kavir, the "Great Salt Desert." Marco Polo describes the region as an area of "utter drought and neither fruit nor trees and where the water is . . . bitter." We found it less inhospitable in the twentieth century.

The near-empty expanse of sand and salt is today crossed by a road paved only in some sections. The only fruit to be seen was carried in the bags of our bus companions or spread out over the dashboard of the vehicle within easy reach of the driver. But where there was any settlement of people, there often grew a lone, spindly, lovingly nurtured tree. Once or twice in a day's travel we came upon a *chai khanna.* At these teahouses the traveler can take off his shoes and sit on carpets spread over the hard, dusty earth. Here he can always order a pot of tea and some bread—the enormous flat sheets of *nan* carried over the arm of the waiter like muslin dish towels. With luck, an egg or two will be available.

The spindly tree might have produced enough leaves to cast a little shade over the carpet. Or a ragged cloth awning would be draped between poles to shield the traveler's head from the sun. This is where we ate in villages large enough to have a small amount of food to sell. This is where, daily, we made new acquaintances.

Even if we had wanted to, we could never sit alone at the teahouses. Almost as soon as we had loosened our bootlaces, someone would come over and ask us to join friends or family groups. Everyone quickly moved babies and baskets and bundles aside so we could squeeze into the circle. We would sit down with legs folded under us, and the introductions would begin.

When there is little shared language, one can at least exchange and understand names, and then the answers to "Where are you from?" and "Where are you going?" Numbers are easy. "How old are you?" was a popular question. Somehow after drinking our tea and passing the fruit basket around, and after a lot of laughter and gesturing and consulting the dictionary, we would all part with some faint idea of who everyone was, and what each was doing that day on the road, and, very likely, the ages of everyone in the group.

Leaving Yezd was quite an event. We gave up the car and bought bus tickets. A half dozen loudly vocal males had to push the bus through the gates of the bus yard and past a mountain of cucumbers piled for sale in the street and on the sidewalk. The motor started and we were on our way, with our feet resting on a cushion of grape seeds as the driver drove and spit seeds in all directions. When not eating, he joined in the prayers being chanted at intervals by his passengers.

The bus had to pause only once for repairs during the journey, and at some point during the cold, star-decorated desert night the driver stopped to sleep for a while in the aisle between the seats. Shortly after sunrise we arrived in the town of Tabas.

Tabas is in the middle of an arid nowhere, but within the boundaries of the oasis grow pine trees and an abundance of date palms. We walked through several large rose-filled parks, around splashing fountains and past swarms of orange butterflies. Enormous mounds of melons were on sale in every storefront and on every street corner. Almost everyone we passed had a dripping melon slice raised to his mouth or a round green melon tucked under an arm or tied to a bicycle. Dates were also plentiful. A young doctor told us that the second major crop of Tabas was, surprisingly enough in the center of the desert, rice.

Tabas, "queen of the desert," contains the ruins of a large ancient fortress that belonged to the sect of the Assassins. Marco Polo tells about these people and their leader known as the "Old Man [or Sheikh] of the Mountain." In a beautiful valley to the east of Tabriz, enclosed by two mountains and protected by a citadel, he built a luxurious garden stored with fruits and flowering shrubs. Palaces of various sizes and forms, decorated with paintings, works of gold, and furnishings of rich silks, were scattered about the grounds. Vessels of wine, milk, honey, and pure water were everywhere. The palaces were inhabited by beautiful women skilled in singing, playing all types of musical instruments, and dancing, especially dances of amorous allurement (probably a medieval version of the modern belly dance). The women were all richly and exotically clothed. The object of establishing this fascinating garden was this: Muhammad had promised that all those who followed his will would reach a paradise where all forms of sensual gratification would be found. The Old Man of the Mountain claimed that he was a prophet and peer of Muhammad and that he too had the power of admitting into paradise all those he favored.

He looked for youths between the ages of twelve and twenty who were skilled in the martial arts

Most of the buildings in Tabas were crowned with a type of masonry windsail, known in Persian as badqir *or "windcatcher." The* badqir *captured whatever breeze moved across the desert town, thus providing some cooling air to circulate in the room below. In Marco Polo's words, "The climate is excessively hot—so hot that the houses are fitted with ventilators to catch the wind. The ventilators are set to face the quarter from which the wind blows and let it blow into the house. This they do because they cannot endure the overpowering heat." Tabas was totally destroyed in 1978 by an earthquake that took the lives of almost all of the people in this once flowering oasis.*

and appeared to possess a special courage. He would then administer hashish to such an extent that when the youth would be half dead with sleep he would carry him into the garden of his paradise. When the youth awoke, he found himself surrounded by lovely ladies singing, dancing, attracting his attention with fascinating caresses, serving him delicate, exotic foods and exquisite wines, until he was drunk with the excess of enjoyment and truly believed he was in paradise. After a week he was again drugged and taken out of the garden. He was given an audience with the Old Man of the Mountain and told, "He who defends his lord shall inherit paradise, and if you show yourself devoted to the obedience of my orders, that happy lot awaits you." Each young man was then glad to receive the commands of his new master and was not at all concerned about dying in his service. With this type of dedication, the young men were sent on missions all over the world to kill whoever was marked for extinction. The service of these disciplined assassins was in high demand. The word "assassin" comes from the Arabic word for the drug hashish—*hashshashin.*

*O*lder citizens saluted us with *"salaam"* as we walked, and the children said "good-bye." Not, we hoped, because they wanted us to leave, but because it was probably the one English word they had learned. In some towns the one word was "hello," or a shrieking "Eeengleesh?" shouted by little children in the general direction of our armpits. Only once did we hear a shouted but dubious "Japaneese?"

Tabas hasn't been a stop on the way to anywhere since the days of the caravans, so we were somewhat surprised to find three other guests at the hotel. They sat in the cool, shady garden behind the hotel, eating melon and playing backgammon. They said they were businessmen from Teheran who had come to Tabas "for a rest." Although fashionably and expensively dressed, they all wore the one-size, style, and color plastic slippers placed for the guest under every hotel bed in every hotel from western Turkey to eastern Afghanistan.

Two of the men offered to take us with them the next day to Meshed in their air-conditioned Range Rover. We couldn't refuse.

*T*he next afternoon, after a lunch of thick yogurt and salad, we sped off into the desert.

(In September 1978 Tabas, a quiet town that grew peacefully in the middle of a vast desert, was so totally destroyed by an earthquake that only a few hundred of the fifteen thousand inhabitants were found alive.)

The terrain was mainly flat sand rimmed by wind-carved rocks and bare pink- and amethyst-colored mountains. On either side as we drove north we passed occasional *qanats* filing toward occasional desert-colored villages, or camel herds parading toward unseen tents. The drive took nine hours at thunderous speeds across the desert plains and around hairpin curves on treacherous mountain roads.

It was late when we arrived in the spacious, thick-carpeted, chandeliered lobby of the Hyatt Omar Khayyám Hotel at the entrance to Meshed. Our Iranian companions managed to look appropriately clean and well-pressed. We managed to look as though we had just completed a hike across the desert, even though we had actually ridden in cool splendor.

Everyone everywhere seemed to be related to, or at the very least a close friend of, everyone else we met. We stopped at this elegant place because one of our companions from Tabas was a relative of the manager. This was fortunate, because our appearance in Meshed was not well timed. It was still the month of Ramazan. The weekend of our arrival was the beginning of special religious celebrations within Ramazan, and Meshed, long a sacred city for Muslims, was bulging with pilgrims. Finding rooms anywhere, we quickly discovered, was impossible. That included the hotel in which we were standing.

It hadn't occurred to us that we might not find shelter for the night. We always had. So, surrounded by beautifully dressed people, we stood in the luxurious lobby, chatting and cheerful and brushing the dust from our clothes.

We could see that some telephoning and a lot of spirited discussion were taking place at the

Near the entrance to a shrine in Meshed, architectural ornamentation shown here is representative of an art form found throughout the Muslim world.

reception desk between the clerks and the hotel manager and his relative, our friend from Tabas.

Soon our companion announced to us that behind the hotel, beyond the swimming pool, and down a gravel path to and through a storybook rose garden, was a villa, once a special place kept for the Shah on his visits to Meshed.

Laughing maids prepared king-size beds for the night and left dozens of thick, soft towels in the tiled bathrooms, where we showered in an unending flow of hot water. We found ice water at each bedside and flowers on the tables and dainty, silver-wrapped chocolates on our pillows. "The Six Million Dollar Man" was effortlessly speaking Persian on the television screen.

All this was something of a shock after the hotels and campsites to which we had become accustomed and before long would once again become accustomed. No rusting iron beds here with one threadbare sheet, no single twenty-five-watt bulb dangling from the ceiling at the end of a frayed cord, no bathrooms that could be safely entered only while wearing boots. There weren't even all-one-size plastic slippers under the beds. Good luck was with us once again.

Marco Polo doesn't speak of Meshed, although he traveled through its province of Khurasan. The town was old long before the Polos passed this way, and it is located only minutes from the juncture of caravan routes from the south, east, and west, as well as north into Russia.

Today, outside Meshed, a seventeenth-century caravansary stands at the crossroads where earlier ones stood as protective islands in the desert and as landmarks. A single, heavy-doored gateway opens into the rectangular mud-brick structure that continues to shelter passing shepherds within its massive walls. Animal smells lingered, and straw and the evidence of recent cooking fires could barely be distinguished in the shadowy interior. From the watchtowers above the high walls we could see distant villages and dry, barren hills rolling to the horizon.

Several meters from the caravansary are the adobe walls of the village of Sang Bast, the third of three successive villages of that name, according to the aged mullah who came out to greet us. The mullah, who estimated his age to be "more than a hundred years," is the village authority as well as teacher and religious leader. This gentleman was slightly deaf and very dry and brown and wrinkled. He was dressed in a tattered shirt and pants, with a tattered white turban wound around his head. He was most dignified.

Stretches of eroding city wall and a mausoleum with traces of blue paint lingering on the inner walls, a minaret, and many scattered bricks are what remain of the abandoned eleventh-century second village. The village, said the mullah, may have been occupied as recently as a hundred years ago until an earthquake tumbled homes and fortifications. His father had told him stories of repelling invaders from the parapets of the second village, nomadic invaders (who came to pillage the towns and carry off the women) with whom the villagers in the present Sang Bast were still doing battle only thirty years ago.

Men drifted out of the village to listen to the mullah, and little boys stopped. The women glanced at us quickly and continued walking, except for one small, sobbing female who saw us and paused and stopped crying to stare at the strangers standing outside her town. Then she pulled her tiny black chador into place, continued sobbing, and scurried on.

Meshed began as a neighboring village to the once-important town of Tus. Tus, then six centuries old, is said to have had a half million inhabitants when the first Mongols rode over the hills and began the destruction of the town. Its collapse was completed—as the collapse of so many other cities was completed—by Tamerlane in the fourteenth century. All that remains of Tus is eroding and blowing as dust back into the surrounding desert: extensive walls, a fortified hilltop citadel, empty watchtowers.

Neither was Meshed ignored by the Mongol warriors, but the shrines were rebuilt or repaired, and the city continued to grow more recently as a center for the wool trade. Since the ninth century it has been a pilgrimage site; only Mecca and Medina are more sacred.

The shrines and burial places to which the Muslim faithful come are those of Caliph Harun al-Rashid and of Ali Reza, the eighth Shi'ite Muslim imam. The twelve imams (descended from

Ali, son-in-law of the prophet Muhammad) are considered by the Shi'ites to be their absolute spiritual authorities and leaders. The spiritual community, it is said, is still led by the twelfth imam who, although he long ago disappeared, "will return at the end of time with truth and peace."

Non-Muslims cannot enter the shrine or pass through the mosaic and mirrored walls of the antechamber of the venerated imam's tomb. But the gilded copper dome can be seen from most points in Meshed.

From the ruined citadel we could see the modern town of Tus and the marble edifice which contains the marble tomb of the poet Ferdowsi, who was born in Tus and died early in the eleventh century.

Around the inner walls of this twentieth-century structure are large high-relief carvings of scenes from Ferdowsi's epic poem, "Shah-nameh" or "The Book of Kings." Called the first history of Persia, the three-part poem describes historical events and recounts creation myths and heroic tales of mythological Persian kings. Written nearly four centuries after the Arab military invasions and linguistic incursions, the poem is best known for having revived the use of classical, literary Persian. For this Ferdowsi is honored.

The caravan route east follows a paved highway from Meshed, past Sang Bast, to the frontier. On the other side of the Afghan border waited another and older time, and few highways.

Farming in Afghanistan has changed little since the thirteenth century. Fields are made ready with animal-drawn wooden plows; seeds are hand-planted, crops are reaped with the ancient sickle, wheat is separated from the chaff by the wind, and, as here, grain is ground by an ox-drawn stone. The yurt in the background serves as this farmer's summer home.

Afghanistan

Crossing from Iran to Afghanistan gave us the feeling that we had stepped even further into antiquity and closer to the world the Polos experienced when they came this way.

The Polos had followed the fifteen-hundred-year-old "Silk Route" along Afghanistan's northern border, along the Amu Darya (the ancient Oxus River), and eventually entered the area known as the Wakhan Corridor. This narrow finger of land three hundred miles long pushes between the Pamir Mountains and Russia on the north, through the Hindu Kush range with Pakistan to the south, and ends in the east at the back door to China.

Officials at the Embassy of Afghanistan in Washington, D.C., urged us to avoid the northern route across their country because it would be "too difficult" and, more importantly, "too dangerous" because of bandits, disease, religious fanatics, and the general uncertainties of desert travel. But as Marco Polo had established our itinerary in 1275, we had no alternative but to follow in his footsteps, difficult or not.

More than once during our journey we felt as if we had stumbled onstage during the performance of some little-known surrealistic play. The Afghan customs ritual was one of those times.

The elderly baggage inspector never sorted out who was entering the country and who wanted to leave. He rushed hysterically from one heap of luggage to another, rapidly opening and closing bags, examining some bags two or three times and others not at all. When he finally despaired of trying to establish who was going where, he threw up his hands, cried, "Finished, finished," and disappeared.

One official had an extended and noisy tantrum when he discovered that the brick doorstop had been removed from in front of his office door. Another wrote camera and money information in his notebook and asked all who came before him if the word "customs" on his sign was correctly spelled.

Thirteenth-century Tartar huts greatly resemble the felt-covered yurts *that one still finds in Afghanistan and China. Contemporary drawing by Sr. Q. Cenni. From Colonel Sir Henry Yules's* Travels of Marco Polo *(1903).*

Opposite, top: *Across the border from Meshad is Herat,*
originally settled by Persians twenty-five hundred years ago.
Alexander the Great destroyed the original city and rebuilt a
new "Alexandria" in 330 B.C.; one thousand years later the
Arabs arrived and introduced Islam to the area. The Friday
Mosque was built in the tenth century. Bottom: *A bakery in*
Herat where nan *is baked in an oven below the floor is not far*
*from the citadel (*right*) that offered protection for the residents*
of Herat for centuries. Pages 106-107: *In a valley of the rugged*
Hindu Kush mountains, along the road between Bamian and
the lakes of Band-i-Amir, we came across a small farming
village where potatoes were being harvested and wheat was
being separated from the chaff, while a group of nomadic
women made a kilim *(a woven carpet). On the main street of*
*Bamian (*top right*) a metal worker is assisted by a customer. A*
*beautiful lake at Band-i-Amir (*center*), situated at thirteen*
thousand feet, was formed, according to legend, by a miracle
caused by Ali, son-in-law of Muhammad. It is called
Ban-i-Khamar, the Lake of the Servant. Pages 108-109: *Deep in*
the Hindu Kush mountains, carved into the wall of massive
rock, stand two gigantic Buddhas. This one (viewed from two
perspectives), known as the Great Buddha, is the world's
largest at one hundred and seventy-five feet tall. The Buddha's
draped covering is reminiscent of a Greek tunic, introduced no
doubt at the time of Alexander. Pages 110-111: *Just south of*
the Russian border is the city of Mazar-i-Sharif, where the
great mosque housing the (alleged) tomb of Ali is located.
Only white pigeons fly in the parks surrounding this colorful
shrine. Page 112: *Faces of Mazar-i-Sharif: a baker stands by*
the oven where round flat breads are baked and his helper
poses with a smile; the butcher awaits his customers for the
day's freshly killed lamb; the teahouse offers a warm drink
and a serene atmosphere to those who have journeyed long
across the northern Afghan deserts.

It wasn't, and all who entered his office dutifully told him so and probably had been telling him so for years.

The official who stamped passports had worked up a routine in which, with each visitor, he reached across the length of his desk for the stamp on the ink pad, stamped the passport, and then—with hardly a glance to his left—flipped the stamp through the air and back to the ink pad three feet away. He never missed his target while we were there.

One of many decorated Russian-built trucks found throughout Afghanistan.

The first bus we boarded in Afghanistan was not encouraging. About twenty travelers—several Australians, some Europeans and Afghans, and us— wanted to go to Herat. We packed ourselves onto the benches and old tires that would be our seats in what, in some bygone era, had been a ten-passenger bus, and looked down at the ground through the holes in the floorboards. The doors had to be padlocked to keep them from flying open, and the brakes obviously were not the best; the bus began slowly to roll down the hill on which it was parked. This presented no problem because rolling the bus down the hill was the only way the motor could be started. Noticing that his bus was leaving, the driver got in and we started toward Herat.

We sputtered along the desert road past abandoned caravansaries and dome-shaped brown tents until the last of the twilight was fading. At that point the driver stopped his decaying vehicle and began to collect fares, holding money in one hand and his flashlight in the other. After some arguing he accepted the previously agreed-upon fares from those of us who had obtained local currency. He then tried to extract much more from those who hadn't anything other than dollars or Persian money. After a lengthy and heated conversation about reasonable currency exchange rates and agreed-upon fares and whether we would pass the rest of the night in the desert or move onward, everyone paid something.

The male passengers, thoroughly irate about the financial discussion, now had to climb out and push the bus in order to restart it. We clattered and sputtered once again into the darkness.

In Herat the lodgings, unsurprisingly, were not of quite the same quality as those at the Meshed Hyatt. Not one laughing maid (women aren't

allowed to work in hotels in Afghanistan) or
chandelier or rose was in sight. We found,
instead, creaking metal beds with no covers, the
dimmest lights possible, and no chocolates on the
pillows. But the sheet on each bed appeared to be
clean, even if the bathrooms unquestionably were
not, and the broken windows let in the cool, fresh
night air and the soothing sounds of horse-drawn
carriages—*gurdis*—passing in the street below. We
found the mismatched plastic slippers under the
beds.

Those who worked in the hotel were delightful,
friendly people. We spent many hours over tea
with the educated and youthful manager, Reshed,
who told us his life story, a story that sounded
like the plot of an adventure film. It included a
wicked stepmother, a politically powerful and
unloving father who wanted to have Reshed
arrested for holding "unacceptable political
views." It included obtaining a university
education that led only to restlessness,
difficulty in finding a job with adequate pay,
and therefore little hope of ever accumulating
enough money to purchase the bride he wanted or
enough to go to medical school, which he wanted
more. We heard similar tales of disappointment
and discouragement from many other educated
young Afghans.

The sunny, beautiful nine-year-old "assistant
manager" of the hotel met us on the stairs the
night we arrived and assured us that his was a
"very fine hotel." He boiled eggs for us and made
us laugh and treated us as though we were valued
friends from the moment we introduced ourselves.
Friendly enough, too, was the dazed-looking
young man who brought the tea and the scanty meals
from the kitchen, burping and wiping the grease
from the plates on his messy apron as he set the
table.

Several ancient cities stood where Herat is
now, including one built by Alexander the Great
after he first destroyed the existing town. The
site was settled by the Persians
twenty-five-hundred years ago and for a thousand
years or more was a major stop on the caravan
route. No longer the center of science and
culture it once was, no longer a simple village,
Herat is not quite modern either.

The water flowing alongside paths and
sidewalks in the *djubs*—small sewer and water
channels—was nauseatingly dirtied with
everything from pigeon feathers to human excreta.
Children played in the water and drank it, and the
adult males washed their faces and hands in it
before spreading their rugs and mats on the ground
to pray.

Camels made complaining noises as they paced
through the broad, unpaved streets to the bazaar
or back into the desert.

Nomads' tents had been placed next to houses at
the edge of town under the watchtowers of a
disintegrating fifteenth-century citadel.

Nan accompanied everything we ate, whenever we
ate, and although once in a while it tasted and
looked like warmed cardboard, usually it was
crusty and flaky and very good. Near the Herat
bazaar we stopped to watch the bread being baked.
Five men squatted around a deep, circular,
clay-lined pit in the bottom of which a fire
burned. The first man dug a handful of dough out of
a pot and rolled it and passed it to the man on his
right. This man flattened the roll into an oval
shape and handed it on to the next person, who
pulled the oval into a thin, broad sheet—like a
dish towel—and patted it onto a wooden paddle.
The fourth man leaned forward, slid the paddle
down into the pit, and slapped the dough onto the
clay wall, where it began to bake. Meanwhile the
final member of the group had been picking browned
bread out of the oven with long tongs, along with
the kettle of water for tea that had been heating
in the depths of the pit.

In our travels we hadn't met many people who
spoke more than a few words of English. In
Afghanistan we were surprised at the number who
did speak it, some nearly fluently—for instance,
Reshed and the young "assistant manager." One
youth called out to us from a shop doorway and
offered to purchase all the clothes we had on our
bodies. Well, if we didn't want to sell anything,
perhaps we would "like to buy some French perfume,
the real thing?" After we talked for a while
longer and then started to leave, the young
merchant called out again to ask if he had used
correctly the word "obtrusive." He had.

We had two things to do in Herat: to obtain a

permit to make the journey across the northern Afghan deserts and to find transportation for it. We located the police commandant, who knew only a few words of English. He telephoned someone who knew more English, and the telephone voice instructed us to cross the courtyard and go to the passport office. The gentleman in this office sent us back to the street to buy a sheet of "official" stationery and a stamp to place on the paper. We wrote, as instructed, our names and our itinerary and our request for permission to follow the itinerary we had outlined. The passport official rewrote our English words in Dari (a form of Persian) and sent us back across the courtyard to the commandant, who went away with the papers, saying something about "checking visas." He never did ask to see our passports, which contained the visas he apparently wanted to check. Twenty minutes later the commandant sent us once more to the passport office, where all the numbers, names, requests, signatures, and approvals were copied into a ledger. Our official paper with the official stamp was signed. We had our permit. Now to find transportation.

With Reshed's help we arranged to go in a truck to Maimana. There was no way of knowing what several days in a truck in an unknown desert would mean, but we would be prepared. The water jugs had been filled. We bought fruits and raisins and pistachios and a fresh fruit-filled cake. And then, after sampling the first tasty cake, we ran back to the shop and bought another one. We also bought butter. Reshed insisted on the butter to go with the cakes. It seemed about as practical as setting forth with a bag of ice cubes, yet the butter never became quite liquid and continued to taste like butter after several days in the desert heat.

Early one morning we went, as requested, to the truck yard. Someone tossed our backpacks into the rear of the brightly painted vehicle and told us to get into the front and sit down. We got in and sat down. One by one, other passengers crawled into the back. Close to an hour later the driver appeared. He started the motor, listened to it for a minute or two, turned it off, and left again. We continued to sit.

The driver was handsome and looked about twenty years old. He was immaculately dressed in the traditional knee-length shirt and full pants, both pale green and spotless, and a dark vest. Over his short black hair he wore an embroidered and beaded skullcap. (After two days of riding through the blowing, drifting sand, his passengers were disheveled and dust-covered. The driver, in the same pale green shirt and pants, remained immaculate.)

At long last the truck was loaded with twenty-two male passengers and Joanne and bundles of food and clothing. The driver returned, and we left Herat.

Briefly there was a road, then a road that was actually a dry riverbed, then a road that was a riverbed in which flowed about eighteen inches of water. And then only desert.

The driver maneuvered his little, Russian-built orange truck as an artist would: flying through seemingly unfordable streams and somehow over trackless impossible-to-climb dunes. He found his way through the night when one section of the roadless, rock-strewn landscape looked exactly like every other section visible in the headlights. His hands moved with a graceful coordination that was absorbing to watch, and he was obviously enjoying his difficult job.

Inside the truck penetrating cold alternated with intense heat during the day's journey. We were surrounded by the aroma of gas fumes mixed with the scent of the ever-present collection of melons, with dust and sand permeating everything. Outside was a different and silent reality: masses of sunbaked, barren ridges, a desiccated land of white sand and sandstone, cracked and waterless gullies and ravines. Nothing moved.

Toward sunset we saw vineyards and pistachio groves on the mountainsides, then rare encampments of nomads near the rare rivers, and camels kneeling at the sides of tents beneath red rock cliffs, waiting for their burdens to be untied and lifted off. Little girls and their mothers, all unveiled and each wearing two or three or more vividly colored, silver-spangled dresses, stirred the evening meal over small fires. Fierce-looking earless dogs guarded the encampments and the herds.

The camera-shy nomad women were proudly visible, but away from the larger towns we often passed an entire day without seeing one Muslim female, adult or child. When we did see one, she would be totally hidden beneath her veil—not even her eyes were visible behind the thick brown or gray fabric of the finely pleated chador. Sometimes we glimpsed only the tips of shoes. We watched these shapeless, ghostlike figures sorting through bolts of fabrics in the bazaars. We hoped that the gaily printed yardage they bought would be used to make gaily printed dresses to wear beneath their somber veils.

On extended bus trips, when we and the male passengers got out for tea or meals, the Muslim women remained on the bus. Crouched behind the seats, they raised their veils just enough so that they, too, could eat.

Long after sunset the truck followed the fast-moving River Murghab into the lamplit town of Bala Murghab, a few kilometers from the Russian border. In Bala Murghab we stopped at a large teahouse for a meal of rice and yogurt soup and shared several pots of tea with the driver and his passengers. Then, leaving the Afghan passengers to finish their tea, the driver signaled to us to get back into the truck. We obeyed, and off we drove on through the town, across the river, through a small wood. We stopped in front of a smiling little man holding a lantern. The driver had delivered us to the doorstep of the government inn.

That night our fellow truck passengers slept on the tea-stained and sugar-encrusted carpets in front of the teahouse. They wrapped themselves in the cloth of their turbans against the desert cold. The driver had decided that we should sleep in warm beds.

We Americans were the only guests at the inn. According to the register, there had been one guest two nights before.

As the town and the inn obviously had no electricity or running water, it was a little surprising, after posing the automatic, routine question, "Is there a shower?" to be told, "Yes." Certain that we had chosen the wrong noun from our limited Dari vocabulary, we nevertheless followed the smiling gentleman and his kerosene lantern to a semioutdoor room. Inside there was a hole in the floor, a plank to stand on over the hole, a twenty-five-gallon drum containing some water, a small faucet at the base of the drum, and an eight-ounce tin cup to transport water from faucet to soapy body. In other words, a shower. We used it with pleasure by the light of the stars which shone through the drafty incompleted walls of the room.

The truck driver said he would return to the inn for us at 6:00 a.m. And he did! We were dressed, ready, and amazed. This was perhaps the one time in the entire journey that we departed from anywhere within two hours of the appointed time.

The road from Bala Murghab to Maimana was not actually a road, but a visible trail, corrugated and horrible, across the wilderness. It was midafternoon when we reached Maimana. Not a living creature was in the streets, but dozens of schoolboy faces appeared at the windows of a classroom across the road from where the truck had stopped. We got out and unloaded our backpacks and water containers and food bags. As we shook hands with the driver and the remaining passengers, the schoolmaster joined his gaping, waving students at the windows. We waved back and entertained our audience by slicing and eating our final pink melon on the spot before striding off to the hotel we had seen a few blocks back.

Time and again, from San Francisco to Maryland to central Afghanistan, we listened to words of warning about the dangers to travelers— particularly non-Muslim travelers—in this part of the world. None of the dire predictions seemed to have anything to do with the cordial, smiling, even protective treatment we received from the kind people we met each day.

Nevertheless, we assumed the warnings must have some foundation. Several times during the journey to Maimana the driver could push his truck no farther. He had to stop and ask the passengers to get out and walk (once for more than an hour) so that the emptier, lighter truck could then climb over the fine, loose sand of the steep dunes of the desert. At the first stop at the first steep dune we started to strike off uphill with our companions; the driver wouldn't allow us to leave the vehicle. Then or later. He gave us his orders

in eloquent pantomime, pointing first to the lonely, desolate landscape, then tracing unmistakable throat-cutting gestures between our ears.

Why, we asked in Maimana, was a man with a rifle seated at the door of the inn? He appeared nightly just before sundown, and we accepted the explanation for his presence: there had been recent nighttime murders of "foreigners" in the area.

Maimana was a quiet, isolated town. We thought it unlikely that we would meet other tourists there. But there they were. There was a constant stream of people past and through our doors at the inn. An English cyclist stopped in to ask for some shampoo and to rest on the edge of a bed while he talked of his travels and his mysteriously ebbing strength. He omitted until the end of his story the fact that he had been living for two months "on bread and water so I could save money." A German couple who lived in Kabul visited us, and a middle-aged ex-Afghan government official sat with us on the carpet at tea time. He told us that he was jobless and wandering through the country and preparing to resume the playwriting he had begun and given up years before.

There wasn't much to do in the sleepy town except drink tea, walk through the empty bazaar, visit with the hotel guests, and watch a group of local women make carpets. It was time to move on.

*R*amazan was now over, and the post-Ramazan festivities began. After we had been told that there would be no transportation in any direction for a while because of the holidays, an eastbound truck pulled up to the inn early one morning looking for passengers. After a mere ninety minutes of fare and destination discussions, then the loading and fueling of the truck, we drove out of Maimana.

This driver was older and not so spotless, and he drove with less enthusiasm than the green-clad youth from Herat and with more than an occasional mashing of gears, but he was congenial and, holiday or not, he was going our way—to Mazar-i-Sharif.

Only a short distance from Maimana, we entered a village where the streets were filled with

Opposite: *The trail from Herat to Mazar-i-Sharif was marked with only the ruts of earlier truck traffic. There were long stretches of tabletop nothingness where the wind had erased all traces of previous travel. Our truck driver continued on confidently, with an intuitive sense of direction and perhaps the sun to navigate by. From time to time the dunes became impossible for the truck to surmount until the passengers got out and walked.*

people and color; a procession was just leaving
the mosque. Little girls, looking like Oriental
princesses, wore quilted jackets over pink and
red dresses; beaded and tasseled hats sat on their
shiny black hair. Little boys were dressed in
bright blue long shirts and full pants and
brighter blue beaded skullcaps, and their parents
were no less brightly dressed in purple and red
and green.

We stopped to buy the inevitable melons and
crossed a bridge that took us away from the town.

In the early hours of the journey we rode past
camel train after camel train. Winter was
approaching, and the nomads had begun to move to
warmer grazing areas. Some of the camels carried
enormous water containers to settlements we
couldn't see. Others had been loaded with folded
tents, cooking pots, jars, and babies in dirty but
colorful clothes.

At the sides of the caravans walked huge and
disorderly herds of sheep led by an
imperious-looking "king" goat, while not far
distant marched the goat herd itself, with an
occasional loner posing elegantly, goat-fashion,
on the face of a bare cliff. A fat eagle soared
overhead.

Soon there was nothing. We left all landmarks
and all signs of life, animal or vegetable,
behind. This part of the desert was absolutely
unmarked. Ruts from the truck tires were erased by
the wind as quickly as they were formed. We
wondered aloud a time or two if the driver could
really know where he was going, with nothing but
the blazing, lemon-colored noontime sun and his
instincts to guide him.

Reassurance came in the form of another truck
approaching us directly over the wavering,
glittering horizon. Our driver indicated that the
truck came from Mazar. The vehicle passed us as
closely as if we had been traveling on a
well-marked city street.

We paused for lunch in Shibarghan, a town Marco
Polo called "plentifully stocked with everything
needful." The oasis, to all appearances, had
fallen on hard times during the last seven hundred
years.

We ordered tea and finished the fruit-filled
cake from Herat. Although we were accustomed to

food prepared and served in a fashion not remarkably hygienic, this teahouse looked dangerously less than clean. Perhaps it was the several men sprawled on the carpets who obviously had some debilitating disease. Or maybe it was just one of those days when we couldn't have faced yet another mountain of rice—the only food available.

Not many hours after lunch the truck tugged itself out of the sand and onto a paved road that took us into Mazar-i-Sharif after dark.

Here, as we unloaded our bags and baskets on a street corner, the helpful driver told us where to find the hotel. *"Bale,"* we replied, "yes." And he repeated his directions. *"Bale,"* again. And we repeated this verbal routine two or three times more. Was it that we didn't look bright to this gentleman? Or maybe he was afraid we would lose our way in the night. Which wasn't too likely, since for ten minutes we had been looking at the lights of the highly visible hotel only several hundred meters from where we stood.

At the hotel the man who cleaned rooms and ran errands immediately turned his broad grin in our direction and adopted us—in fact almost pounced on us. "Do you want a drink? Maybe a beer? A soda? Coffee? Tea? Are you hungry? Do you want to eat?" He recited the entire dinner menu. "Shall I wash your clothes in the [sewage-filled] *djub?"* Anything. He would take care of it any time we met— which was often—during the following few days.

In the next days this dynamic gentleman helped us to find our way around Mazar. He began his food and beverage recitations before we had even brushed our teeth in the morning, and he told us which bus to take for the seventeen-kilometer ride to Balkh to the south of the River Oxus.

Balkh fell to the Persians twenty-five hundred years ago and grew again, to be seized by Alexander the Great and later, in the seventh century A.D., by the Arabs. An important part of the caravan route and a focus of Islamic culture, this once great Central Asian city was devastated by the warriors of Genghis Khan.

In 1222 the city was easily captured. The residents were ordered to leave the city limits and to remain beyond the walls until they had been counted for the census. In the meadows outside

The town of Mazar-i-Sharif (Tomb of the Exalted) is built around the shrine to Hazrat Ali, son-in-law of the Prophet Muhammad. The first shrine was built over a hundred years before Marco Polo came this way. Not far from the blue-tiled edifice along one of Mazar's broad streets is an open-shed bakery, where a pancake-size flat bread is baked in a breadbox-size oven.

Balkh, Tartar horsemen, said to number one hundred thousand, surrounded and slew the entire population of more than one million people.

Marco Polo, fifty years later, despite the destruction, comments on the size and the grandeur of this ruined center of commerce and learning:

> *Balkh is a splendid city of great size. It used to be much greater and more splendid; but the Tartars and other invaders have sacked and ravaged it. For I can tell you that there used to be many fine palaces and mansions of marble, which are still to be seen, but shattered now and in ruins.*

Since the nineteenth century Balkh has been little more than a village bordered by cultivated fields and enormous ramparts, now slowly eroding. The walls are so high and extensive that it is possible to examine easily only limited sections of them.

The pleasantest part of the visit to Balkh was a social call. An ancient gentleman with a wonderful deep laugh called to us as we passed his shop. He was a metal worker and samovar craftsman, and he invited us in to share—naturally—a melon he had just sliced. We entered the cluttered room, removed our boots, and squatted on the spread carpets to begin our visit. At once the doorway and soon the entire tiny shop was filled with beaming males.

Our host, who was born on the other side of the River Oxus in Russia, demonstrated his ability to write our names with Roman letters. We all spoke about birthplaces and our homes, the distances between our homes and his, and modes of travel to these places, in the very few words understandable to all of us in Russian, Persian, and English, and with pictures sketched in the air by a dozen pair of hands, and always with lots of laughter.

After posing in the center of the shop with his tools and a friend for an exquisitely dignified photo, our host accepted our thanks for a lovely afternoon. We departed to continue our explorations.

From Balkh and Mazar-i-Sharif, the Polos continued on to the east through the passes of the

Opposite: *Along a street of Balkh a camel follows its master between the mud walls that protect the town's vegetable gardens. This ancient cultural center is today a village of a few thousand people; it is famous for its melons and noted for growing the finest quality hashish in central Asia. It was here that Alexander the Great married Roxane in c. 328 B.C. Balkh then continued to prosper and grow until A.D. 1222, when Genghis Khan came and murdered its entire population of one million people. Tamerlane tried to rebuild Balkh in the fourteenth century, but it never attained its earlier grandeur.*

Wakhan Corridor and on to Cathay. We had reached Mazar in mid-October, and the extremely high mountain passes farther along the route to China would already be snow-filled and impenetrable.

Our journey had come to an end for now, and we started back toward the twentieth century on a plane to Kabul.

*I*n our adventurous raid upon this ancient world we tried to capture its image as Marco Polo may have seen it. The dozens of notebooks we filled and the thousands of photographs we took became the fruits of our effort. After four months of traveling, we began to feel at home in this unfamiliar and sometimes terrifying environment. Someday soon when the snows melt and the back door to China swings open we will again head for the "roof of the world," making our way across the thousands of miles to the Gobi Desert and on to Peking in the footsteps of Marco Polo.

Band-i-Amir, the "Grand Canyon" of Afghanistan.

Epilogue

It was fortunate that we were able to make our way along the Marco Polo trail during 1975.

In the following four years earthquakes caused massive destruction and killed tens of thousands of people in Turkey and Iran.

During 1978 the revolution in Iran was fermenting.

In late 1978 a Soviet-backed coup deposed the government of Afghanistan.

In January 1979 the Shah was forced out of Iran and a revolutionary government was installed.

In November 1979 Americans were taken hostage by Iranian militants at the American Embassy in Teheran. As of April 1980 the hostages, all connected with the United States Government, were still not released.

In early 1980 Soviet troops invaded Afghanistan.

Acknowledgments

$\mathcal{I}$t is with great satisfaction that I acknowledge Joanne Kroll, my co-author and fellow traveler. After returning from a sixty-thousand-mile bus trip through Central and South America, and with only six weeks to make the necessary personal arrangements, she agreed to go halfway around the world to follow in the footsteps of Marco Polo. Joanne provided much-needed assistance in the planning and execution of the expedition and was an inexhaustible source of knowledge on all subjects. It is to Joanne that I am deeply indebted also for the many thousands of words that she added to the text, helping to make it a definitive description of our journey.

In addition I am grateful to my son, Rick, for his keen humor, strong back, and for the tolerance he showed for his father. I extend a special recognition to Eleanor Braun, Isaac Rehert, Bette Taylor, and Nancy Susman, all of whom read and criticized the manuscript and provided constant support.

I must also acknowledge the help of the hundreds of people in the embassies and the government agencies of Italy, Israel, Cyprus, Turkey, Iran, and Afghanistan, and of the thousands of others along the way who helped with a smile or a hand pointing in the right direction. I am indebted as well to the employees of many companies that helped with information, equipment, and services. These include Nikon Cameras, Pan American Airways, Jan Sport, Silva, and Alpine Designs.

Lastly, I would like to express my gratitude to my mentor, Frank Shor, associate editor of *National Geographic,* who died shortly before our trip began. He and Jean Shor had made a similar but uncompleted journey in 1948. It was their book, *After You, Marco Polo,* that was a key inspiration for our travels in 1975.